Too Much

Also by Tom Allen:

No Shame

Too Much

TOM ALLEN

HODDER*studio*

First published in Great Britain in 2022 by Hodder Studio
An imprint of Hodder & Stoughton
An Hachette UK company

1

A CIP catalogue record for this title is available from the British Library

Hardback ISBN 9781529397437
Trade Paperback ISBN 9781529397444
eBook ISBN 9781529397451

Typeset in Bembo MT by Manipal Technologies Limited

Printed and bound in Great Britain by Clays Ltd, Elcograf S.p.A.

Hodder & Stoughton policy is to use papers that are natural, renewable and recyclable products and made from wood grown in sustainable forests. The logging and
manufacturing processes are expected to conform to the environmental regulations
of the country of origin.

Hodder & Stoughton Ltd
Carmelite House
50 Victoria Embankment
London EC4Y 0DZ

www.hodder.co.uk

*For Mum – always strong and always
knowing what to do with the flowers*

Introduction

We were never the sort of family to have something like this happen because, aside from anything else, we were the sort of family who had always been very much alive.

My dad died at the end of 2021. It was a shock, especially as I had only just moved out of my parents' home a few months previously, and I was still finding my feet in my first relationship. It felt like this should have been an exciting time of new beginnings.

Dad and I were very different and at times I worried I could be too much for him. For example, I was brought up to resist any unnecessary dramatics. For my parents, this was an uphill struggle.

'For goodness' sake! The Scout leader doesn't hate you, he doesn't think you're a fool – you just fell over in the mud and he lifted you out – that was all.'

'*And* picked me up by the back of my coat and *carried* me across the finish line because I was so slow *and* everyone was laughing.'

'You're being dramatic. Not everyone was laughing. Most of the others had started heading home.'

'That's even worse!'

'Well . . . maybe the Scouts aren't for you.'

As anyone who read my last book knows, I have always felt different, 'better' even, than everyone else. I have always loved being formal, by which I mean wearing suits, studying etiquette manuals and setting the table elaborately. As a small child I didn't have many friends, mainly because I would tell the other children that I was an emperor.

In contrast, my dad was quite a direct working-class man from South-east London who had worked as an electrician, a car salesman and a coach driver. Not that he couldn't still be sensitive to people's rudeness and the coarseness of the world, though, and would exclaim, 'Charming!' sarcastically in his London accent if he found himself affronted. He had the best heart and, rather than poetic mantras, and in contrast to my quasi-'posh' outlook, would say things like 'Shove it!' to dismiss anything stressful. On certain occasions, when trying to impart to me not to overdo things, he would even use the phrase, 'Look, Tom, there's a difference between scratching your arse and tearing the skin.' Which was charming, indeed.

As you'll see in the essays that follow, it was advice I probably should have heeded more.

Despite my flirtations with imagined grandiosity, I finished my last book with a sense that maybe my life had only been half lived: I was thirty-seven and had never been in a relationship, I could barely drive a car, I hated the suburbs (namely my home town of Bromley) and I was living at home with my parents with a desperate sense, which I'd carried since childhood, that I should stay at home to protect them. Somehow, me being there meant, in my mind at least, that I could protect my mum, Irene, and dad, Paul, from invisible foes, and at the same time cling to the hands of the clock and stop time moving forward (alas, owing to my mother's penchant for more modern interior design, most of the clocks are digital).

Now, as I write this new book, the changes wrought do seem to warrant the term 'dramatic'. I am sitting in the back bedroom of my own house, which is firmly and very happily in the suburb of Bromley, just three minutes from my family home. I have a boyfriend, Alfie, who looks out at me from my phone screen, and I write this wearing jogging bottoms and a hoodie because, actually, they are quite comfortable. It dawns on me that maybe I'm not that different to everyone else after all, and I find that prospect truly terrifying.

Despite our differences, I have come to realise that Dad and I showed we cared about each other in different, less obvious ways. What follows here are snapshots in time - moments when I realised that dad was with me, whether I was in suburban Bromley or somewhere around the world. What I have come to know is that he was there more than I realised and I hope that in some way he always will be.

'You can never have too much love'

Dad said this to me once whilst he was making me some breakfast. Probably a bacon sandwich. It struck me as surprisingly sentimental, but then he could be like that sometimes.

I

This is your dad's funeral, not Eurovision

'Oh, I'm sorry to hear you've not heard back yet . . . Well, the pandemic has slowed everything down. And, of course, it is December so they tend to be rushed off their feet . . .'

'Like inn keepers in Bethlehem, I suppose?'

' . . . Cappuccino, please. I will have a look for you, but I'm not in the office at the moment – I'm in Pret A Manger. The phone diverts to my mobile you see— No sugar. That's great . . . No, nothing else . . . Is it this card terminal here?'

'Sorry?'

'No, no, it's me, sorry! Just paying for my lunch! Never know which card machine, err . . . That's great, thank you! Sorry, as I was saying, sorry it's taken over a week. It shouldn't take that long. I will check through and chase up what's happened. Rhod will give you a call – he's in charge.'

The wait to hear back from the coroner had taken longer than expected, so we'd had to call the number in the pamphlet Mum had been given.

'Is Rhod the coroner?'

'What, Rhod? Oh no! He's at a nativity. His daughter's play-ing one of the wise men, but it's a big deal, as last year it was all on Skype. Rhod just oversees the office I'm in.'

Eventually, Rhod did call. It was after lunch. A chicken salad sandwich. He was reverent and low-voiced in a matter-of-fact sort of way, and he must have to speak like that all day. It being December, I thought how strange their Christmas parties must be, and wondered if they spoke like this even when wearing party hats. It occurred to me that I didn't really know what the coroner was meant to have done, apart from confirm that Dad was definitely dead. My brother, James, put him on the loudspeaker and rested his phone on the table so Mum and I could hear what he said.

'Err, yah, it was a – err – myocardial infarction, basically a heart attack. Classic furring of the arteries.'

'Would he have been in any pain?' asked James.

'Err, no – probably would have been quite instant. He certainly wouldn't have known what happened.'

I looked down at the crumbs of the sandwich on my plate.

At the time of writing, it has been some months now since Dad died. It didn't suit him at all. He was much more the type to fix the dishwasher, or to climb onto the roof to move the satellite dish in bad weather, or fit a new kitchen at the age of seventy-eight. Maybe, he'd drive me to a gig in Cambridge, or he'd grow his own vegetables, or carry twenty-five kilos of water-softener tablets to my front door. But dying suddenly of a heart attack? On a train, causing the service to be cancelled and subsequent trains to be delayed? No, that didn't suit him at all.

In fact, the last text he sent me was to ask, 'Are you in? I think I should come and bleed the radiators in your house – I could hear them the other day. They make a banging noise when they need doing.' A strange final word. He never did get a chance to bleed them, though.

All the drama suited me much more. With a love of formality and high ceremony, I was finally presented with the perfect moment to exercise the utmost in decorum, though somehow this sort of propriety didn't seem as much fun. Whilst formality in the form of a table centrepiece or a folded napkin can have a playful quality, in death, this formality acted for us like a handrail to steady us as we traversed the precipice between normality and deep sorrow. Work colleagues suddenly wrote solemn, heartfelt messages, exuberant exclamation marks and emoticons were lost from friends' text messages and neighbours 'expressed their condolences' like diplomats presented at court.

In the aftermath of this seismic shock, a routine rapidly emerged, which included sitting around a table and oscillating between tears and talking, or more often than not, talking in that high-pitched voice that feels like it could crack at any moment and teeter over into tears. People came knocking at the door and would come in and time was busied with making more tea and opening more tins of biscuits, and my bitten nails couldn't quite undo the plastic strip bound around the lip of the tin. We were frantic, trying to make sure everyone was catered for, and exhausted from endlessly popping to the shops to 'just grab some milk'. My advice to anyone in this situation is to abandon hot drinks altogether and buy several bottles of brandy and serve it neat in tumblers. The bottles are recyclable, the glasses go straight into the dishwasher and the brandy helps much more with the emotion.

Friends of my dad went from being the allied gatekeepers against the harshness of the world, as I had always seen them, to suddenly being devastated and vulnerable themselves. The neighbours I had grown up knowing like family were no longer fearsome protectors who kept an eye on our house when we were away, but were just normal people who wept openly whilst sat round our coffee table. The men who seemed to be in control and able to laugh boldly at life, some of them the same age as my dad, revealed that they weren't really adults after all but just like children, scared and confused by the world and how it treats us.

Many of them had known grief themselves, losing partners and even their own children. The familiar look they had in their eyes, which I'd always seen, was something that I now understood more. The realisation that when they had talked too much or focused on something trivial, like the weather or the leaves clogging their guttering, it had been their way of trying to distract from the sadness they carried through their every day.

They came to our house and cried in the doorway before tiptoeing across the threshold. Strangely, they all removed their shoes, either in respect for the carpet or to make themselves seem a softer presence in the house. They seemed even more like children, as they reminded me of my brother's friends from the neighbourhood who would come round to play when we were young. The bending over to undo the Velcro like a short quick bow – down, then up – followed by a rise and fall as they used the front of one foot to remove the back of one shoe and then the other: a momentary ceremony to acknowledge entering the house. My grandmother, prone to worrying about everything, would call after my brother, 'You'll break the back of those shoes if you keep bending them at the back like that!'

As these grown-ups entered our home – a place I found myself painfully still referring to as 'Mum and Dad's' for the first few days – the shoe-removal ceremony repeated. It reinforced that here they were as children, still playing as adults, trying to do the right thing, trying to work out how this game should be played.

A list of legal formalities and death admin – 'Deadmin', if you will – mounted up like a tax return for a life; a form of accounting for which you can have no preparation. You realise these nods to tradition and to-do lists are all you have to bolster you up and stop you from saying to everyone, 'Please excuse me so I can try and come to terms with what's happened and maybe cry and hide here in this cupboard for a few years.'

There was one moment that we had been fully prepared for by countless friends, and that is the ordering of death certificates. 'Get at least twenty!' they'd said. 'Everyone wants one!' What they would want them for, though, seemed unknown. Like a certificate to put on the wall saying 'You Passed!' but meant quite literally.

Once the formal hurdle of hearing back from the coroner was complete, the list continued and seemed to be endless. It included telling the government to stop paying his pension, telling the bank and the insurers to close accounts, taking his name off the joint account, changing the name on the account with the internet provider, phone, cable package, TV licence, council tax, water, gas, electric, car insurance, speaking to an undertaker, planning a funeral . . .

It is strange to be surprised by death, especially as television seems to be filled with murder. Not on the Food Network perhaps, but the other channels are chock full of *Poirot* and *Inspector Morse* and *Midsomer Murders*. Reruns of detective series, which at one time seemed dramatic enough to warrant a prime-time slot, are now hidden away on smaller channels during the day. You might even catch an old episode of *Hetty Wainthropp Investigates*, starring the outspoken Patricia Routledge detective who walked so Brenda Blethyn's Vera could run. These daytime death-fests are interspersed with adverts centring around donkeys on building sites, baths that have doors on them and people telling you to plan and pay for your funeral in advance. These morbid characters tend to be in their early sixties and stand in a neat kitchen with Venetian blinds. They talk directly down the camera while merrily peeling a boiled egg and tell you, 'Oh yes, I've paid for my funeral!' as they rinse their hands, tickle a cocker spaniel and wave at the postman. How well organised these people always seem – they manage to achieve so much!

Alas, despite being very organised, Dad was always sceptical about being sold anything, and so didn't leave instructions or a funeral plan. He had occasionally broached what he might like to happen: 'Just throw me in a box, and if we're abroad, don't bother flying me back – just chuck me in the sea.' It was as though planning ahead like that would seem self-indulgent or flamboyant – dramatic, even. How could you sit around assuming how people would remember you when there was guttering to be fixed and water-softener tablets to be purchased?

It seems strange that someone who was so matter-of-fact and direct about things would ever be lured in by something as dramatic as one's own mortality, as though death would be too over the top for him. In my mind, if Death had come knocking on the door, he would've just told him where to go and carried on with mending the washing machine.

It is a cliché to write about the superhuman strengths we perceive in our parents. Dad was extraordinary – of that I have no doubt. He grew up in one room in Penge after his own father (in Dad's words) 'pissed off'. His mum, who I never met, was ill for much of her life, and she died in Dad's arms in the late 1960s. Despite the ulcers on her legs, she still worked as a cleaner, and she still walked up to Anerley Town Hall every Saturday morning to collect the one-pound child support from her estranged husband. 'I'm sorry, Mrs Allen,' the clerk would say, 'I'm afraid no money has been paid in this week.' It was resilience rather than sentimentality that prompted my dad's mum, on turning that corner from Croydon Road into Penge High Street and walking straight into her estranged husband who hadn't paid the pound for his son's upbringing, to smash him straight round the face.

Dad grew up with nothing except the love and support of his mum, his cousins and grandparents in a house on Jasmine Grove. And that was very much Dad's mantra: the effort you expend on looking after one another knows no bounds. And when it comes to love, it is infinite; you can never give too much.

People say you have to make sure you tell people you love them while they are alive. In the days after he died, I found myself wishing I had said this to Dad, wishing I had hugged him more. My friend Darren Styles very quickly put this to bed, though: 'He knew already all you wished you said,' which I think was the best advice I received during this time. If I had suddenly started hugging Dad, he probably would have been so surprised it would have hastened a heart attack, or he would've shouted, 'Get off me, for gawd's sake!'

It's complicated to explain to my American friends how British people express their feelings. Americans are, by their nature, earnest and polite, but in the UK, if someone likes you, they can be more abrupt with you. The ruder they are, the more intensely they trust and care about you. Calling someone some profanity is, for many friends, the highest form of flattery. Dad wouldn't go quite that far, but he showed love by helping us; he was devoted to us but sometimes it was in an abrupt way.

If he felt relaxed enough to say to you at the end of your dinner party, 'I'm going now. I'm bored of you lot,' it meant he thought the world of you. We once had people round to our house, and Dad got tired of hosting, so appeared in the living room carrying the guests' coats asking, 'Which one of these is yours, then?' Mum was absolutely horrified. In our supersensitive world, this behaviour seems obscenely impolite but to Dad this was just him showing you his true self. He would help anyone who needed it, whether it was a lift in the middle of the night, or a trip round to fix your oven/boiler/bird house. More than this, the main way he would show his love was by making you a bacon sandwich, even if you didn't want it. Vegetarians and vegans would visit, and still a toasted bacon sandwich would be put down in front of them.

I kick myself now for pushing away Dad's help. It felt like it was stifling – like every time he cut the grass or took out my recycling without me asking him to, he was saying he didn't trust me enough to look after my own house. If only I could have let myself be vulnerable enough to just let him care for me. Not that he'd always make it easy.

'Take in those cushions on the garden chairs!' he'd bark.

'They're waterproof – you don't have to.'

'Yes, but they'll last a lot longer if you look after them.'

'But I don't want to have to fuss about taking them into the shed and then getting them out again all the time!' And then, like a child complaining that they can't stay up late like their friends at school do, 'None of the neighbours take theirs in. You don't—'

'You're being absolutely ridiculous! Take a look at yourself. It's no bother at all, is it?' I'd stand there, feeling chided, in the hallway of my own house.

Now the story has ended, I realise that there was no use in fighting it – that was just how we communicated. People don't always show that they love each other by hugging and tickling a cocker spaniel, because real people don't live in a catalogue or an advert. Real people are perhaps more likely to show their love by bickering senselessly over weatherproof cushions, for fear that anything else might be too dramatic; too much.

Dad wasn't part of a generation who had time to curate their existence while videoing it on their phones. They didn't use filters to enhance how beautiful they were and they didn't feel it necessary to proclaim their moral superiority across social media. He was born in 1941, so anyone of a similar age no doubt felt they were lucky to survive the Second World War – they were busy living their lives!

In fact, some of my dad's friends were so bad at filming themselves that during the lockdown, when video messaging was their only way to see one another, they sat in front of their windows with the light behind them and thus silhouetted themselves – I'd walk in to find Dad with his iPad, looking like he was chatting to a group of people being interviewed on *Crimewatch*.

'Is there a risk it looks more like a flyer for a dance night?' my brother asked when I presented him and Mum with the funeral invitation I had designed. The initials of the French phrase '*Répondez s'il vous plaît*' seemed flamboyant in the circumstances.

'Well, I could remove the clip art, if you think? Maybe the font could just be something simple, like Times New Roman.'

'Do you think people will RSVP? It's not a film premiere.'

'I just want all the information to be in one place – so people don't misunderstand what time it starts, et cetera.' Strange to say 'et cetera' out loud in conversation. 'And if we're singing a hymn,

I think we should send out the lyrics in advance – so people can rehearse.'

'Tom!' interjected Mum. 'This is your dad's funeral, not Eurovision.'

'I know, I know. I just want it to be perfect.'

The sun shone on the December morning we went to meet the undertaker, and for once, we arrived early. I have inherited my mum's ability to be late, which has always been in contrast to Dad's punctuality. One of the reasons I've always been so daring in terms of timing is that if you arrive early, you suddenly end up with time that has no purpose, those extra minutes suspended in the ether, for what? Skulking? James, Mum and I sat in the car as our new, more compact unit and watched people on Eltham High Street go about their early-morning chores in the cold winter sun. It was so odd to think that people could carry on as normal when all we wanted to do was say to them, 'What are you doing? Don't you know our dad has died!' Either that, or there was a sorrow, a pity for them: how blissful they seem to be, busying themselves when maybe this same sadness awaits them too.

Nowadays, parlours are only used for ice cream and funerals. Once a staple of every middle-class home in the nineteenth century, parlours were a signal of moderate affluence in that they showed to the wider world that you had enough rooms that you could afford to keep one for best. Usually, they were a small space crammed with heavy furniture and heavy drapes, elaborate patterns interrupted by doilies, antimacassars and aspidistras, all steeped in Victorian chintz and archaic formality. Now stripped of their old-world decorum, people tend to use the terms 'lounge' (which to my mind conjures up images of airports and hotels) and 'living room', which, while a peculiarity given that surely all rooms are for living in, seems apt since parlours are now reserved for the dead.

This funeral parlour had just been renovated, so it was glistening in greys with bright spotlights in the ceiling. I liked the way that they had tried to make this a space that felt cared for, tasteful and not stuck in the past.

'Oh, it's beautiful! Like a show home!' said Mum excitedly. Show homes have always pleased my mum. When I was a child, one of her favourite Saturday-afternoon adventures would be to drive us to a new housing development and pretend that we were interested in purchasing one of these new dwellings. Dad wouldn't be interested, but I jumped at the chance. Going for a drive was a classic pastime of my parents. It wasn't that they were headed anywhere in particular, just being out in the car was exciting enough – usually the countryside, where things were spacious and luscious green. I was pleased to be out going somewhere but I couldn't understand why we would be driving in the opposite direction to where all the people were – the buzz of the metropolis with its fast-food outlets and traffic jams. A simple pleasure, I realise now, that was based on escaping the stresses of the town – oblivious to me as a child – the noise of traffic and, basically, just other people. My parents spent a lot of time just escaping 'people'. It was something just to be moving, to be free! Until the next set of traffic lights.

I enjoyed the night-time drives especially, usually taking place on a Sunday, when Mum would suggest we go for one just 'to get out of the house'. She and I, in the Nissan Bluebird, cruising round the mean streets of places like Shortlands and Green Street Green, playing the *Very Best of Elton John* cassette loudly. 'Pinball Wizard' would blare out, and as we stopped at traffic lights, passengers in other cars would turn to look at us, surprised to see we weren't young hooligans but the owners of a small mobile disco happening between a mother and her nine-year-old closeted son, singing along merrily to 'The Bitch Is Back'.

My favourite of all drives, though, was when a trip to a show home was included. We would travel to somewhere like Sevenoaks to view the one house in a development decorated to look like people lived there. Mum would create elaborate ruses that 'Yes, we've put our house on the market and we're looking to downsize.' The saleswomen with their pencil skirts and suspicious demeanours would sit through another rendition of 'Yes, we are seriously interested in your houses and would dearly like a sales brochure and also free rein to look round your show home.' Dutifully, they played along and asked Mum about part-exchange options, to which she'd respond elusively with, 'Well, I'd have to speak to my husband about that,' and the look on the saleswoman's face gave the impression that maybe this husband was as imaginary as the home on the market.

'Would you like me to show you around—'

'No, no! No, thank you. We are happy to just have a wander,' Mum would snap, not wanting to have to extend our ruse further. Mum really just wanted time to live out the fantasy that this sparkling new house and the immaculately placed bowls in a kitchen free from clutter with ample work surfaces was hers! 'Oh, you know, it's just good to get ideas, isn't it?' she'd whisper to me as we crossed the threshold and stepped onto the bristling new doormat, the smell of new carpet hitting us in the face. I knew she really meant to say, '*Why?!* Why can't we live like this?!' If only her life was immaculate like the woman in the housing developer's brochure. As though there were people in the world who managed to live a life where there was always enough room on the work surface, there was never any clutter and there was time to peel a boiled egg and look out the window at the postman. Everyone, I think, on some level longs to be part of this imaginary league.

Clearly, the undertaker had a flair for interiors, as it was true, the funeral parlour – or funeral lounge – did look like a show home, albeit one that played very sombre music. Elgar and Fauré mournfully on repeat.

A young, bespectacled man appeared from a back office, smiling. 'You must be here to meet Matthew! Would you like a tea or coffee?' He was sprightly and a few years younger than I expected him to be, younger than me certainly, and a reminder that the older people we once looked up to for these roles eventually retire and die so that, in turn, our generation have to take over their duties, and thus we become the older generation ourselves. And so the world turns.

'Oh, Henry makes a terrible coffee.' Matthew, similarly young, bounced out of a side room marked *Chapel of Rest*, which somehow implied to me that perhaps he used it for his own rest and had just woken up. This wasn't true of course and he didn't look at all sleepy; in fact, quite the opposite. I immediately noticed how shiny his shoes were and knew instinctively the interior design must have been his work. In fact, I suddenly felt like I was in an interiors programme and about to begin an appraisal of the decor. 'There's a great flow to the space – you really feel held in this entryway.' I could imagine Michelle Ogundehin saying, 'This photograph of a hearse on Blackheath Common really takes you to the heart of what this building is about!' Or if it was an American interiors programme like *Selling Sunset*, someone with bright white teeth would exclaim, 'Oh, gorgeous funeral home!'

The two young men smiled amiably, and Henry disappeared into the back office-cum-staffroom to prepare our beverages. I wondered what that staffroom was like. Surely it couldn't be the same as just any office staffroom, with tea bags drying by the sink and a pinboard of Christmas party photos? As with the coroner, I couldn't help but wonder where undertakers would go for their Christmas party. Would they keep their top hats on and travel in one of their stretch limousines or even a hearse?

We sat in grey velvet chairs around a large desk while Matthew sensitively talked us through the various packages available and, to his great credit, was calm and upbeat and then serious when he needed to be. He never tried to up-sell any part of it.

'Would you like to talk about casket handles for Dad's coffin?' he asked amiably. What a strange question that seemed. 'No, not really,' was what I wanted to reply.

'Is there an option where we can shove him in a box and throw him in the sea? That was his wish, you see.' But alas, this was not something on offer.

'This is our most straightforward package,' he said, holding up some pages from a brochure, 'which I'd recommend.'

He talked us through every element of what needed to be arranged, from flowers to post-funeral refreshments. I sometimes find that people scoff at ceremony, wanting to hide away from overly formal behaviour and seriousness, finding it embarrassing or phoney and at odds with our casual modern lives. However, the formality of a funeral makes sense at a time when emotions run high, as somehow it becomes a structure to hold you. My teenage obsession with etiquette and ceremony started to seem justified; I was just a young person wanting to be a grown-up and taken seriously.

On the day of the funeral, we gathered in the kitchen and managed to eat croissants and knock back a brandy. 'Dad's here,' someone said and so we looked out of the window to see the slow cavalcade as it appeared around the corner with Matthew walking out in front, wearing a top hat and carrying a cane. To my mind, it had all the hallmarks of the musical *Oliver!* and suddenly, it dawned on me that I would have been a great undertaker. It's everything I love: formality, ceremony and top hats. And then I realised what a terrible undertaker I would be, as no one wants to say farewell to a loved one led by someone like me who would be clearly enjoying the performance too much.

We greeted Matthew on the garden path with glazed-over eyes but trying to keep it together because you can't say 'good morning' to someone and burst into tears. How strange to start every working day shaking hands with small huddles of people crying, all of them so sad to see you. It is the opposite of being a comedian, where people are pleased to see you (except for that time I did a gig in Woking).

The funeral limousine arrived behind the hearse. They are a very specific kind of limousine in that they are not like the ones you see film stars arriving in at film premieres – the sort they get in the film *Big*, where they go round the city with their heads poking out of the sunroof. That wouldn't do for a funeral, I suppose.

But they are still grand in their own way. Instead of the L-shaped sofa and minibar that limousines have for hen parties, these stately cars have rows of seats in them, which can accommodate three people per row. My brother and I sat either side of Mum. With them holding three people in a row, it does mean the person in the middle has to shuffle across when they get in, which turns the experience into something more reminiscent of a night out when you try and save a few pounds by getting the maximum number of people in an Uber.

There is a lot of bowing of heads and doffing of top hats that goes on from the undertakers. I felt very awkward that I didn't know what it all represented and felt like I should join in, but then kept doing it at the wrong time, which seemed even less respectful, like a child trying to copy the grown-ups.

I don't remember a huge amount from the ceremony other than sort of wanting it to be over. The church service was conducted by our local vicar, Jonathan, at the church on the corner of my road. I was worried about the singing of a hymn because people feel embarrassed about singing these days and often don't know the tunes. Jonathan recommended, since it was still Christmastime, 'O Little Town of Bethlehem', which was much more recognisable for the masked congregation to sing. We said our goodbyes at the lychgate of the churchyard. Someone in an old souped-up sports car outside the pub opposite kept revving their engine. At another time, I might have regarded it as a neat metaphor for the rudeness of our modern world, and part of me regrets not going over to tell him to '*Shut the fuck up*'. However, feeling as I was that day, it all seemed part of the turning of the world, all of us just at a different point in our day, in our lives.

We waved goodbye to the hearse as it took Dad on his journey to the local crematorium. As it turned along the road where I live, we all realised that Dad would go past my house; Dad's last job to check that the recycling had been put out and collected.

The wake followed, though why it is called 'a wake' eludes me, as it is literally the last thing the deceased will be. Lots of people came up to say hello and pay their condolences – coach drivers, who had travelled from as far as Wales and Newcastle to our little suburb of South-east London, because Dad had helped them in some way, like helping them overturn a traffic fine. Strangely, it made me feel like the whole funeral was like a wonderful party, and for a time I forgot what the purpose of the whole event was.

We held the wake at the golf club in the same dining room I had once theatrically wheeled a dessert trolley around as my first job. We had decided to play a slideshow of photos of Dad on the television there. I have always found photographs unbearably sad. Snapshots in time, moments in a life captured quickly in happy times without thinking that one day the subjects of the photographs might no longer be with us. These two-dimensional versions the only thing we have to confirm our memories of how they looked. Searching through old drawers of photos, I was surprised to see that they showed Dad to be a man – just a man. In flared trousers and with a bit more hair, they showed him as a younger man, and in the black-and-white versions frayed at the edges in albums that had lost their binding, they showed him as not yet a man but just a boy.

Because technology is infuriating, we couldn't find a way to get the slideshow of scanned photos to play on the screen until I tried to AirPlay them from my phone. For a reason I could not fathom, this system kept faltering. 'It's an LG television and you've got an iPhone, so they don't get on,' someone said. 'Well, do you think they could maybe make it up, given the circumstances?' I wanted to shout, but who would I shout it to? The situation meant that occasionally the television would default to showing the live TV stream, meaning that photos of my dad as a young man were punctuated by half an episode of *Flog It* (complete with finalé kick) and later on in the day, scenes from the film *The Great Escape*. Mourners remarked that they didn't realise Dad had been involved with either of these things.

The whole experience of losing someone feels very disorientating. In this confusion, I have found there can be a mix-up in the subconscious because so often we talk about *losing* a loved one. 'I'm so sorry for your loss,' people say, and the mind distorts this when we are resting and vulnerable to be a literal loss, as though they went out one day and somehow found themselves in Epping Forest or Watford and couldn't work out how to travel back to us.

There is a cruel dream I've had since Dad died. I had the same experience when my grandmother died too. In the dream, I stumble upon a strange house – maybe it's a cottage in a wood or a flat on the other side of London. In any case, I am surprised to be there; it's not somewhere I know at all. There seem to be other people milling around casually, and then I am doubly surprised to find that Dad is there. He gets up out of the chair to greet me, as he always did, and I am taken aback, but fundamentally so relieved to see him. I feel that he's about to offer me a bacon sandwich. I am so relieved – suddenly, it all makes sense! I tell him that we've been so worried about him, that everyone's been phoning – we've just been crying all the time. But this explains everything! 'Oh, you didn't need to go worrying about me, Tom! I've just been here. I guess I should have told you.'

'Oh Dad! Wait till I tell everyone! They'll be so pleased to know I found you.' And then the dream ends.

I have always had a fear that if I started living my life too much, there would be a price to pay. I felt like I needed to be at home, making sure everyone was always safe. Then slowly I started to make leaps away from the family home in buying my own place, getting a boyfriend, going on a holiday. It seemed like such an indulgence to go abroad and to the Caribbean. Somewhere I'd never dreamed of going before but as restrictions around the pandemic allayed, it felt like the right time to do it because who knew when we'd get another chance?

I also bought Mum and Dad some theatre tickets for when I was away – *Only Fools and Horses the Musical*. I bought them four so they could take friends. 'No one's around, though, Tom!'

'Well, just go on your own then,' I said dismissively, only too familiar with how they resisted me spending money on them when actually sometimes I just wanted to give a gift. It was for the Tuesday night.

Alfie and I spent the first day of our holiday on the beach drinking piña coladas and running in and out of the warm sea. We even got caught in the rain at one point, just like the song. It was brilliant. I had been exhausted with work, so I was looking forward to just doing nothing and that was what we did. The evening grew dark at around six o'clock and a tropical storm was coming in so we sat in the room. Me reading. Him napping. I'd kept my phone in the bedside drawer all day to avoid getting caught up in messages and emails.

I snuck a quick look, though, as he slept. I saw a missed call from Mum. She would just want to hear what we'd been up to. Which was nothing. Maybe they wanted to tell me about the show. My brother picked up the phone.

'Oh, hi, Jay – you OK?' I said brightly.

'Not really, no.' My brother was serious. He sounded so grown-up. A freezing-cold feeling spread over me as I instinctively braced for bad news. 'Dad was on the train with Mum – and he had a heart attack . . . and' – voice breaking now – 'yeah, he's gone, Tom. He's gone. Dad died.'

I cried so openly that Alf came rushing out and he just hugged me. They'd been on the train to the show. They'd been running for the train. Dad went to put his mask on and pulled a strange face, and that was it. The carriage was empty except for a man called Russell who came to help. A cord was pulled, an ambulance was waiting at Grove Park station, Russell gave him CPR, the paramedics worked on him for forty-five minutes – the same as they would have done in hospital. The British Transport Police sent a car to collect my brother and blue-lit him from work to the station, but there was nothing to be done. A police officer rolled up her coat for Mum to kneel on to say goodbye. 'He wouldn't want you to ruin your holiday!' said Mum on the phone, as if I could stay there.

It was late, and everyone was in bed in the UK. I lay awake in the darkness as the storm lashed the room. The warm Caribbean air filled up my lungs. Lightning flashed and thunder banged loudly. I stared at the ceiling fan in the darkness. I still had to bleed those radiators.

'It's cold enough for a handbag'

Dad would say this when it was cold even though the phrase itself didn't make any sense. He had never, to the best of my knowledge, carried a handbag. Also, I have never heard it as a phrase as part of the lexicon of Cockney or London slang. It doesn't really mean anything at all, especially as a handbag doesn't bring any warmth. I suppose the real meaning is that not everything in life makes sense.

2

A salmon brothel

Dad liked to spend time in my new house. He liked the way the trees on the road dappled the sunlight, he liked the way the roses looked in the garden and he liked the way it had been decorated by the previous owners. He found it bizarre that I might want to redecorate it or change things around too much. The previous owners did a fantastic job of renovating the property and adding a new kitchen and redecorating it, so much so that I found it quite overwhelming at first. I think I was scared of having my own home, having spent so long living with my parents. I had dreamed of how I might decorate my own space, but when it came down to it, I was paralysed with fear. If I did suggest making a change, Dad would grimace. 'Why would you want to change it? It's lovely as it is! You might start messing around with things and mess it all up.'

'Well, I'm only trying to put my own stamp on it.'

'Oh fine, don't listen to my advice – you never do anyway.'

'I always listen to your advice!'

And then he'd shake his head and say something like, 'Oh yeah, it's cold enough for a handbag,' which didn't mean anything. It was a nonsense phrase he'd say if things seemed illogical.

Alfie and I were waving our friend Emily off in her car. She'd stopped by to pick up the keys she'd forgotten and had a coffee with us. It was a sunny day and the beginning of spring as the sun came through the trees opposite. After a year of living in the house, it was mornings like these when the house felt most like my home.

'You are living in our old house!' boomed a voice coming from an older lady on the pavement walking past Emily's car as it pulled away. In a way, quite frail, the woman still managed to have the energy of someone much younger, marching with a sense of great importance – her tone almost admonishing in its directness.

'That's our old house!'

'Oh, really?' I said, brightening once I'd processed what she was actually saying.

'We lived here many years ago. The paving is still the same?'

'Yes, well, I think so – I've only lived here for about a year now. It's taken a while to settle in but I like—' I didn't get a chance to finish.

'I'm Esmé and this is Archibald. We lived here for a long time. We're both quite old!' she said smiling warmly and yet with the same directness. White hair coiffed above her head in a way that was traditional and timeless while wearing a ski jacket for practicality and warmth. She had an ability to say something positive while giving the demeanour of someone you wouldn't mess around with – I imagine she was used to speaking very directly and would take no prisoners at a town-planning meeting if there was talk of a new housing estate.

'I was very sorry to see that, more recently, the owners had decided to try and make it all very modern!'

'Well, actually I like old things so I'm hoping to put things—'

'I see you have steps at the back of the kitchen?'

'Yes, well, I was very fortunate. The previous owners made a lot of changes to make things nicer.'

'I used to have a rockery there!' with a tone which suggested, 'Of course I did! Anyone with a brain would have a rockery there!'

Archibald, her husband, stood by her side, somewhat more fragile and wearing a ski hat, and using not a walking stick but a ski pole for balance. 'We were very happy here!' he said sweetly. Two octogenarians in skiwear, like they had been stuck up a mountain for forty years.

Despite their confident chat, they were vulnerable as they found themselves on the brink of visiting not just their old house but also their memories. Lots of people might be only too keen to get rid of unsolicited visitors, but at moments like this, I am entirely my dad. It was always his pleasure to be the most welcoming you could be in a situation like this. He might even put on his posh voice. He would not wait a moment before inviting them in and so I did the same. 'Would you like to come in and see it?'

It occurred to me that the slippery steps up to the front door might prove dangerous for them to climb, and I wondered what I would do if they fell or if Archibald had a heart attack. It wouldn't be such a happy house for them then. I'd have to wait ages for an ambulance to arrive and I knew I'd blame myself forever that I caused it by inviting them in. 'Shut up your worrying!' I could hear Dad saying.

Standing at the threshold, Esmé pronounced, 'Yes, well, I had a Victorian whatnot here and a grandfather clock – and we had pink carpet everywhere! Did you put the wooden floor down yourself?'

'No, it was the previous owners. I think it makes it seem quite light and—'

'Terrible problem with rot at one point,' murmured Archibald, breathless from ascending the few steps leading up to the front door.

'After we left, there were huge signs put up saying *Keep Out* and scaffolding was up for months. I think there must have been rot?'

Esmé posed it as a question, but I didn't know how to explain to her again that I had only lived in the house for a year, so how could I possibly know? We paused a moment in the hallway; me wondering what they might quiz me on next, them transported back in time to see if the place matched their memories.

Then in the silence, Archibald rasped, 'I see you've taken away our glory hole?'

A silence descended.

'I'm sorry, what?' Alfie's eyes widened, the only part of his face he allowed to show how much he was laughing inside.

'The glory hole! At the top of the stairs!' Archibald lifted his ski pole to gesture upwards, which seemed to bring the idea to mind even more vividly.

'You had a glory hole at the top of the stairs?'

'Yes!' said Archibald. Esmé looked on, beaming, no doubt lost in a fond reverie.

'Oh right. A glory hole.'

'*Yes!*'

'. . . Was it, err . . . popular?'

'Popular? Oh yes, very,' said Esmé.

'We used it for whatever we wanted, really,' Archibald chimed in.

'Well, I'm sure.'

'You exposed the window on the landing?'

'Well, the previous owners did . . .'

'Oh yes, that was our glory hole – you could put whatever you wanted there.'

'In the glory hole?'

'Yes, we used it to store luggage but really it could be used for anything.'

The idea that Archibald and Esmé had set up the halfway landing as some kind of sex dungeon did cross my mind, but then I had a distant memory of the word being used to describe an untidy storage space and my instinct to laugh subsided. 'Come through and see the sitting room!'

Standing looking out of the back window, Esmé surveyed the garden. I felt quite proud of how neat I'd kept it and how the shrubs I had inherited from the previous owners seemed to be surviving well. Being a chronic people-pleaser, I was sure Esmé would be just as happy too and praise me for it.

'Oh, you've changed my garden totally!'

'Well, actually it was the previous owners, but I would like to return it to perhaps a more traditional-looking garden – it's quite square at the moment. As you can see, I've just put in a vegetable bed.'

'Oh no,' said Esmé, quite firmly. 'I should get an allotment for that.' She responded as though I had asked her opinion about whether I should put in a vegetable patch.

I wanted to say, 'No! I'm putting it there! I've decided,' but being a people-pleaser, I just nodded and said, 'Yes, right.'

The use of the word 'should' felt like a remnant of a much more direct, 'doesn't suffer fools' bygone age. A time when people presumably had less time for the 'sorry's and 'would it be OK?'s of our era. There was no malice in Esmé's suggestion; at the same time, it was not a question, but an instruction. It made me wonder if I had wasted too much time in life always trying to be indirect as some sort of oh-so-polite British maxim. Maybe I've always wanted to make myself smaller. I could imagine Esmé being irritated by my constant 'Sorry to trouble you, but would

you mind if I possibly took the trouble of using your toilet?'
type of talk.

It also seemed so strange to me that I would go on a waiting
list to secure an allotment, a distance away from my house, to
grow vegetables in, when I could just open my back door and be
right there.

'I should grow something that climbs!'

'You know these houses were built in the Victorian era by
a journeyman and rented out,' said Archibald, taking a seat –
uninvited – his hands on his ski pole, like the elderly father at
the bank in *Mary Poppins*. 'The rector of the church, he took
one for his mother-in-law. Oh, and the money they made from
selling hymn books meant they could build a whole new church
opposite Sainsbury's!'

'Oh really?'

'But then she died – well, they all died in turn, of course.'

'No, Archie!' said Esmé. 'Tell the story of the burglary!'

'You were burgled?'

'No – well – I received a phone call from the police saying
I'm very sorry to report that you've been broken into, and so I
rushed home, and there were lots of cars outside and so the police
came with me and inspected the property. Turns out the people
opposite had called the police as they thought they saw people
moving around in the rooms – but we eventually realised . . . the
movement they saw was just branches from the tree opposite,
reflecting in the windows!'

'Oh heavens!' I said to play along with the story, even though
deep down I wondered if this wasn't a waste of police time.
Strange how Dad and I enjoyed the welcome reflection of the
trees in the dappled sunlight, whereas at one point, their reflection had been interpreted as literal intruders.

'We moved here with our children, but of course, they went off to university and then it seemed like we had too much space, so we downsized,' said Esmé, smiling. 'We were very happy here – it's a very happy house. I missed it terribly. In fact, for months after we sold it, I would walk past and simply cry.'

'It's a very happy house,' reprised Archibald, tenderly.

'We go to the Bull's Head for coffee, but it was empty this morning! Perhaps people have finally learnt to economise.'

'Yes, perhaps.'

'We had some money from my mother,' said Archibald continuing with the history lesson. 'She lived here with us for a time. But we had to economise too. We held our son's feet to dangle him off the top of the stairs to put the top of the wallpaper up. Thank God he got it right first time! But oh yes, we decorated all this ourselves!'

'Oh, that is impressive,' I said, suddenly aware of how emotional this revisitation might have been for them; a moment of tribulation, trying to get the wallpaper up, and then laughter that they managed to get it done without injury. So many moments: some trying, some laughable – all finished now. And then seeing me, the new tenant, trespassing in the palace of their memories. I could imagine them surprised that I couldn't see their memories every time I looked up the stairwell.

'But for us,' said Esmé, suddenly very sincere, 'this area is full of so many ghosts.' She smiled, and I felt somewhat sad. It was like when the sun goes in for a moment on a bright sunny day. The mood briefly altered. The memories of a family life flashed across her face. I felt unworthy in a way to be living in their space myself, without a family, at times so unsure of whether I belonged here.

It crossed my mind that I might soon find out that they were both in fact ghosts themselves and had died in some sort of glory-hole skiing accident years before.

'I suppose you wouldn't be interested in buying the old lantern we had hanging here in the hallway?'

'No, Archie! He's already got one!'

'Actually, I might quite like it – I do like old things.'

Archibald slowly lifted himself from the chair as Esmé declared, 'We must leave you now,' returning to her directness. 'Half-a-mile walk and half-a-mile walk back – that's enough for us. We are quite frail, you know.'

I was inclined to disagree. I showed them out, and they began their slow walk off together. The morning sun shone through the trees and made reflections on the glass again. More ghosts to fill the house. A very happy house indeed.

I decided to plant my vegetable patch. Esmé's advice that I should get an allotment made the act seem defiant somehow, as though I was shouting after her, 'You'll not tell me what to do in my own home!' The truth is, I am always being told what to do.

I still feel like I am rebelling against the 'advice' from Mum and Dad about what I should be doing with the house, whether it's putting my own stamp on the interiors, or just general maintenance of the water softener. 'Red? Oh, I wouldn't paint a room red – are you sure?'

'Yes, Mum! It's by Farrow & Ball – it's called "Reading Room Red". And I want that room to be my reading room – a library, if you will.'

'Paint it red and it'll look more like a brothel than a library.'

'Actually it's more of a salmon when it goes on.'

'All right then, a salmon brothel.'

Why do I find myself justifying everything I do even though I am a thirty-eight-year-old adult with his own house?

Dad would be similar in his instructiveness but even more direct: 'The garage is certainly *not* broken!'

'Yes, it is, it's—'

'It isn't, the clip needs to be switched when it's closed so you can lock it.'

'Yes, but it isn't locking, is it? Because the bars don't even go across when the garage door is closed!' Suddenly, I sounded like a child again, whining in my difficulty to explain what had actually happened with the garage door without the appropriate garage-door terminology. Before buying the house I had no need to even think about the complexities affecting garage doors and why they don't always close. This was combined with the sense I had that I didn't deserve a house, never mind a house with a garage door and a water softener – who did I think I was? I felt like I should be back living in my childhood bedroom at my mum and dad's.

Their house is a few minutes away by car, so Dad could often pop round. He would arrive with water-softener tablets when I hadn't asked him for them, the twenty-five-kilogram bag heavy in his arms as he trundled down the short driveway. A bag that would be heavy for anyone, never mind an eighty-year-old man. 'Open the door, please!' he'd shout in a clipped voice as he gestured with his eyes to me to open the garage door. I didn't need to worry about opening it, as, because of the faulty bar across the clip thing, it was basically already open, flapping in any wind that happened to whistle around. I was also annoyed at him for getting the tablets for me, as though it was a gesture to silently say, 'See! You can't look after your own house.' He was right, of course – I had run out of the water-softener tablets.

Garden cushions continued to be a source of great consternation. Left by the previous owners of the house, white, waterproof and square, they fit snuggly on the plastic woven sofas and armchairs that seem to be the fashion for suburban outdoor spaces now. Gone are the white plastic chairs which seemed so glamorous in the early nineties, which seem to have been relegated to swimming-pool lifeguards.

Outdoor seating generally was very important to Dad. The garden was a bonus room: a place to read the paper in the sunshine, or to peel potatoes in the warm glow of the sun, using the newspaper to catch the offcuts. It was a room where he could tend to his vegetables, or on occasion, have his friends round for a coffee, particularly during the latter stages of the lockdown when three guests were allowed in the garden and that was the only permissible way for him to catch up with Dave, David and John. The four of them discussing vegetables and what they'd been reading in the paper and making fun of one another like teenagers, not the eighty-year-olds they were.

The idea of eating outside seemed so flamboyant when it first entered our family life when I was around eight or nine. Barbecues were all the rage in suburban gardens in the late eighties, a time to show off the new white plastic garden furniture we'd purchased. As soon as the weather turned to sunshine, charcoal and firelighters had to be purchased along with sausages and burgers to be cooked atop the coals. Then, after the initial excitement, barbecues seemed like too much effort, what with the patience required to wait for them to heat up, the risk of them not cooking food enough and then the exhaustion of scrubbing the bars free of the charred detritus afterwards. Eventually, the barbecue was left to rust in the shed, and we took to cooking as normal, in the kitchen and just taking it outside.

It seemed so continental to be sitting in the early-evening air, even though the sun would have moved to the front of the house by this time. 'We face the wrong way! If only we had a south-facing garden,' Mum would mourn. 'If we ever move again, that's going to be the most important thing. I am going to make sure we live facing the right way.'

Sat in the shade of our house in the cool, the table would be set in the back garden and we would parade the various dishes of whatever we happened to be having that night. As I got older, I was determined to increase the fuss level back up by serving food on wooden boards and salads in large bowls tossed with Filippo Berio olive oil, tomatoes fanned out on a separate dish. It all felt like a step too far, but my parents would dutifully put up with my over-the-top shenanigans with a salad dressing.

The weather was grey and cold in the garden when I decided to start planting the vegetable seeds. But as I approached the chosen bed, it dawned on me I didn't know what I was doing beyond the instructions on the back of a seed packet.

The faux-wicker garden furniture sat on the patio, the cushions hibernating safely in the shed. The furniture's plastic strands, once woven neatly together, are starting to fray as they snap in old age or get picked at by birds in the day. Dad would have put a tarpaulin sheet over them to protect them in winter.

I found bamboo canes at the back of the flower beds and tied them together at the top to make a frame for sweet peas to grow up. I didn't have any twine, so made do with the withered bits of string still attached to the poles from their previous use and a piece of old ribbon attached to the handle of a basket which had arrived at one point as a gift.

I decided that sweet peas, normal peas, carrots and leeks would be the best to plant. They were the ones Dad would plant each year, and so they seemed most fitting. Greens, runner beans and radishes could also be grown, but it felt like it was still too early for them. The small carrots that Dad's garden would yield would occasionally be brought in on late-summer evenings and they tasted so much more intense than shop-bought carrots – a flavour I didn't even realise was possible until tasting it in this intensity.

His vegetable patch was a small rectangle he had in front of the lounge window, which he was fiercely protective of, especially in the face of menacing slugs and snails. It was something he had been taught how to do in the back garden of Jasmine Grove in Penge by Charlie, his mum's adopted father, who had taught him about runner beans and how to establish bean poles so they would grow high and abundant with their orange flowers.

My own attempts seemed paltry by comparison. Dad would often try to teach me about it, and I could remember thinking at the time how I should be listening more intently and how one day I'd regret not paying more attention – these thoughts managing to drown out what Dad was saying. My internal guilt monologue cruelly turned out to be the one thing that stopped me from engaging in Dad's teaching more.

Making a vegetable patch of my own is something I feel might be part of my mourning process – a sort of active grieving, the sort of thing people do in books. I didn't really cry at all. There were a few times when it first happened, and a few times when I realised he wasn't just on a trip, soon to be coming back, or at least just popping in with some water-softener tablets. I kept the flowers sent to his funeral in the hope they would break down and become compost to put on the soil and make the whole thing complete. It didn't work like that, though, as the tough stems of the lilies took longer than I expected to break down.

Based loosely on the seed packet instructions, I realised that it wasn't necessary to place each individual carrot seed in the soil exactly 2.5 cm deep, but that a trench roughly that depth could be made. I did it with my bare hands and it felt nice to be touching the earth. In fact it is actually great to get mud under your fingernails and in the creases in the skin of your hand. I drizzled the seeds into the trench and then covered it over before I began on the trench next door, this one to be filled with seeds for spring onions.

I heard his voice in my head, as clearly as if he was there with me. 'Not too close together . . . You want to give them space to grow . . . Cover them over . . . Now leave them and hopefully, if the sun comes out, they'll come through in a few weeks . . . but just leave them for now.'

I looked down at myself, and then heard his voice with mocking love, even clearer now. 'Look at this dope! Out planting in the garden and he's wearing his three-piece suit!'

That evening, I went to see Mum for dinner. The house seemed strange still, so odd that Dad wouldn't be coming in from the other room to say hello. The new bin my brother bought her for Christmas stood by the side door, which is the main door we use to come into the house. The lid is on an automated censor, so it made an odd mechanical whirring sound when you moved near it to signify that the lid was opening. There was nothing inside as it had not been switched over to from the old bin, and it looked so pristine it seemed a shame to sully its stainless-steel body by filling it with rubbish. It's a bin Dad will never use, which seems sad, but it also felt odd to think mournfully of a bin. Dad would have also hated the automated lid. 'This effing thing!' he would have shouted, saying 'effing' in case the neighbours were listening.

It sits at the end of the kitchen island Dad built. He installed the entire kitchen. They bought it on a whim one day in Homebase. They quite liked it, so they asked the assistant if there was more information available.

'It's being discontinued, so you can buy the whole thing – £1,500, including the oven and the extractor fan.' Mum and Dad had turned back to see a family perusing it, and so, in panic, and thinking they were on the path to a good deal, without measuring it, they told the assistant they'd buy it there and then.

What was not clearly explained was that, as a discontinued ex-display model, they would have to dismantle it and take it home themselves. My brother had to go with Dad to carry it out through the goods lift and load it into the back of a van that Dad had borrowed from his mate Tony.

It was a modern design of kitchen, light wood and clean lines. It did not, however, fit the space required. It sat in the garage for over a year while they worked out how best to get it fitted. And then Dad, aged seventy-eight, decided he would do it. Somehow, he managed to find a space for every part of the kitchen, including the double oven and the tall units with the sliding pull-out shelves which my mum had seen other people have in their kitchens and that she so desperately coveted. 'Oh, if I had those, it would just make everything so much easier. I could see what was at the back of the cupboards – no more finding a Christmas cake from 1987!'

Dad was not a kitchen fitter. He was a coach driver. But he certainly had skills and he was in no way intimidated by the idea of fitting an entire kitchen alone. He could take on any task he set his mind to.

'This effing flooring!' he would screech as he tried to lay the herringbone tongue-and-groove floor panels that he and Mum had chosen, largely because they were on special in the flooring shop. Dad did lay the floor, but it took him a lot of stress as he didn't have the training and he didn't have the equipment. My brother, a tiler by trade, despaired that he hadn't been consulted in the process, but Dad didn't want to be a burden to him.

So Dad did fit the kitchen, and he did fit the floor too. It might not have been perfect and it might have caused him no end of hassle but he did fit it. There wasn't the high finish that a professional would have achieved – there was no backing board fitted to the back of the island unit, and the work surface either side of the oven doesn't align, but only me, their particular, detail-obsessed, precocious son would notice them and shudder.

The toaster sits on the counter under a cupboard, but Dad would insist on the toaster being moved out to hang off the edge of the work surface so that the heat rising from it wouldn't rise up and burn the underside of the cupboard. 'Then it's not fit for purpose!' I wanted to scream at them, but I knew it was too much to say – the achievement was there in actually getting the kitchen out of the garage and making it manifest here.

Mum's insistence that the pull-out cupboards would be the answer to all of their organisational needs was somewhat ill-founded. Yes, now we could see where everything was, even at the back of the cupboards, but they were still without order. It didn't seem to bother them in the same way it did me, but there was no logic as to why the furniture polish and the crisps should live together next to each other in the cupboard, which also housed the boiler. The drawer containing medicines also contained keys to the garage, chewing gum and matches. The herbs and spices were aligned between glass bowls designed for holding crisps and stacks of old credit card statements and cheque-book stubs. It was an order of things that was perplexing to my brother and me, but somehow, after nearly forty years of marriage, made sense to Mum and Dad. A thermos flask next to a vase for flowers and the new J-Cloths would drive my brother and me to distraction.

Standing in the kitchen – the product of my dad's labours – it felt empty now.

'Shall I order a curry?' I asked Mum, food being the best distraction from any kind of emotional pain.

'Oh yeah, sure!' Mum said enthusiastically. 'Are you cold?' My mum is frequently cold and has been known to have the heating on in the middle of summer. The house feels like the Sahara Desert throughout most of the year.

'Yes, I am actually,' I said.

Mum returned with a cardigan. 'Here you go. Try this on – it's your dad's – might be a bit big on you, though.'

I had forgotten that there was still a wardrobe full of his clothes upstairs. 'They remind me of him, cardigans – he always loved wearing them, didn't he?' I pondered.

'Does it smell of him? I sometimes hold his shirts to see if I can still smell him.'

My dad didn't really have a distinctive smell, but I suppose there is a sense of him about the cardigan. It's not overwhelming, though.

Over Christmas, I had been staying with Mum when Rob Beckett had asked me if I fancied a walk with him. We have done a lot of walking these past few years, especially during the lockdown. The long, frosty winter of the year before, with its bleak last-minute cancellation of Christmas and the sense that the pandemic would never be over, had only been punctuated by the government-permitted, once-a-day meeting with one other person for a walk. The parks and open spaces we'd walked through had become gradually more and more churned up by the thousands of extra walkers who had been forced to take up walking as their only pastime and social activity during that endless winter.

A year later, and walking with Rob still feels like an escape from the real world. We talk about what we're worried about, and it makes the world seem a bit more bearable. On this occasion, it felt like a good time to escape everything that had been running through my mind, but I didn't have the right shoes for a muddy park. Rob always has the right pair of shoes – most of the time he wears his light blue and pink pair, which have a sole that stretches beyond the base of the shoe, so it looks like he is wearing a fishing trawler about to go on a Pride parade. Apparently, they are the best walking boots on the market.

'Oh, your dad had a pair – he hardly wore them. I'll get them for you,' said Mum as I was thinking of wearing yet more inappropriate clothing for outdoor pursuits.

I don't like to wear anything too attention-grabbing for sporting activities – it is the one time I don't want attention. I am not, after all, a professional walker (if that is even a job). Mum came down the stairs brandishing Dad's brown leather boots that came to the ankle. They were ideal.

It was only when we were halfway round the park that I realised they seemed to be making a slurping noise. Looking down, it was quickly apparent that the sole was coming loose, at first just a little bit and then before I knew it, the sole was only attached at the front and the boots were more like a pair of flip-flops. My very own winter hiking flip-flops.

Just as I was pointing out to Rob that, according to my mum, my dad hardly wore them, the sole became completely detached from the shoe and I was suddenly wearing nothing less than a leather sock in the middle of a muddy field over half an hour's walk from home.

'Yeah, Mum says he hardly wore them – I can't think why . . .!' We laughed and carried on the walk regardless. It was good to be catching up.

We are surrounded by ghosts. The memories bring people and moments back to life so that they run concurrently with our present day and never really leave us – the fruits of the work people once did, the wisdom they happened to pass on, the shoes that break in the park.

I slipped and skidded alongside Rob as we travelled on through the bright yet eery winter's light, the mud underfoot, the chill in the air – the day cold enough for a handbag.

'If you can't improve on the silence, keep your mouth shut'

Dad was taught this at the technical high school he went to in Penge. At the time he relayed it to me, probably when I was in my mid-twenties, it felt impossibly harsh. Now as I've got older I realise it was as much about appreciating the peace and quiet; time to think, to reflect and to listen.

3

Patricia Routledge wouldn't
have to go into the playground

'Look, the thing is,' said the ringleader, glancing at her nearest friend, 'we've got something to tell you.'

I gulped. What was it? They seldom acknowledged that I was even there, never mind deciding there was something I needed to be told. 'We've decided.'

'Yes?'

'We don't want you hanging out with us any more.'

Perhaps the hardest thing I have ever done is survive Year 6. Everything was changing: my dad had lost his job, I was expected to start growing up and get ready to go to secondary school and now the girls at school had friend-dumped me. They had been taken to the hall for an assembly with the district nurse who visited our school from time to time. It was a special assembly based around periods and becoming a woman, or something like that – I couldn't be sure. Whilst they were in there I had been forced to go and hang out with the boys in my year, but I didn't know them at all. I just sat and watched them play Pogs (a game where you try to flip a small plastic disc by throwing another small plastic disc at it in order to try to win more plastic discs). It seemed so pointless.

I had always wanted to be friends with the girls and not the boys, and for a lot of the time they let me sit with them. I felt like

I could finally be myself with them – talking about handstands and attempting to play a game of French Skipping (where a piece of elastic was held taut round two sets of legs while the person in the middle had to jump under or on top of the elastic in a series of elaborate sequences). We might also discuss that week's episode of the television series *Blossom* where the lead character got to wear different hats and dance on her dad's grand piano and also had the impossibly glamorous privilege of having a phone in her bedroom.

On returning from their secretive assembly, the girls had changed. I didn't know if it was the assembly that did it, or maybe this announcement had been a long time coming and the assembly was just the moment they had been looking for. It was a warm, sunny lunchtime, and we were sitting on the grass. The girls sat with their legs to the side, which was all the rage at this early point in Year 6, wearing their red-and-white striped school dresses (red-and-white gingham was no longer fashionable in the September of 1993).

The girls' appraisal continued. 'We just think you've changed, and we don't want to hang around with you any more.'

I was dumbfounded.

I wasn't accustomed to dealing with conversations as straight-forward as this. 'But . . . but why?' I said, very shocked. I had been on the brink of a handstand.

'Also, your breath smells,' chimed in another one.

'And your jumper – how often do you wash it?' said another.

'I don't know. My mum does it—'

'Well, you need to know: it smells.'

'Of farts,' joined in another girl.

'It does,' chimed in another.

'Yeah,' the others said, nodding. This was the worst lunch ever. I started fiddling with my hands, circling my forefinger around my thumb. 'Why do you always do that thing you do with your hands too? It's so annoying.' It felt like I couldn't do anything right. I didn't have the language to explain what I felt other than the word confusion.

'You've just changed,' said one of the sorority.

'Yeah, you've changed,' pitched in another.

'We're going to spy on the boys,' said the ringleader, 'and, just so you know, you can't come.'

I had nowhere to turn. I was totally isolated as I watched my ex-friends cartwheel off into the distance. One of the girls came back to get some water from the water fountain and stopped by where I was sitting, still dumbfounded and confused. 'You know, Tom, I actually don't think you've changed, but what can I do? I'm powerless – Pauline is my third best friend – I can't stand up to her. She'd kill me. She's too powerful.'

'But—'

'I'm sure you understand,' she cut me off.

The rejection from my school friends hurt me deeply, but I got the impression that I shouldn't be so sensitive about things, and I had to just get on with it. Isn't that what growing up is all about? However, as with all emotions we would prefer to bury, they have a habit of resurfacing somewhere else. In this case, it was at home.

Things were stressful there, as my dad had recently been made redundant by the car dealership where he'd worked as a car salesman for twenty-five years. It was the back end of the 1992 recession, and the economy was still reeling from the fall-out of the collapse in the pound when Britain had to withdraw from the European Exchange Rate Mechanism. Even at this age I somehow made myself aware of financial markets. One of my favourite toys was a pretend briefcase. The car dealership unceremoniously told Dad he was to be made redundant, despite his loyalty to the two generations of the family who owned it. Dad was devastated after a quarter of a century's service, but it taught him, and me, the valuable lesson that deep down, hard work and loyalty seem to be forgotten where other people making money is concerned.

The fear that my parents would have to sell our house hung over us like a terrible, dark cloud. For Mum and Dad, the house represented more than just a place for us to live. It was everything they'd strived to achieve. They'd not had any help from anyone to get where they were – my dad working every day as hard as he could, coming from one room in Penge, leaving school at fifteen – so this house with a garden was everything to him, quite literally. There was a lot of pressure on us as a family unit, and I struggled to find a way to tell them that on top of everything they were going through I had also been dumped by my entire friendship group.

It was after school and I was watching TV before we had tea. My dad asked me to go and get changed out of my school uniform so it would keep smart. Sitting in front of that week's episode of *Blossom*, I didn't want to get changed – what was the point if my uniform apparently just smelled of farts?!

'What are you talking about? Go and get changed.'

'No!'

'Thomas!' my mum said, looking up from a baking sheet of oven chips, alarmed that I was answering back to my dad – something that was absolutely not tolerated in our house.

'Go and get changed, right now!' my dad said.

'Shut up! I don't want to!' And I ran to the downstairs toilet – or 'cloakroom' as my mum insisted on calling it, despite none of us having a cloak, which I lamented. I quickly stood on tiptoes to lock the door behind me.

Eventually, I heard my dad behind me. 'Open this door immediately!' he demanded, shaking the handle. 'Open it right now!' I sat there defiantly. 'I won't ask you again!'

'Shut up!' I shouted back.

'Thomas!' my mum pleaded angrily.

'Right, that's it! I shall take it off the doorframe then!'

'Thomas, what's the matter with you?' my mum screeched.

'I'll go and get my toolbox,' Dad announced to Mum.

I heard him walking away and going out to the garage. I used it as my moment to escape, so quickly unlocked the door and ran upstairs. My dad saw, turned on his heel and followed me as I ran up the stairs as fast as my little legs could carry me to the sanctuary of my room. He caught up with me as I crossed the threshold, about to throw myself on my bed dramatically. He grabbed me by the wrist, spun me round and shook me by the shoulders.

'Don't you *dare* talk to me like that again!'

'I'll . . . *sob* . . . call . . . *sob* . . . Childline!' I said.

'Yeah, go on then,' said my dad, knowing there was no way I would have the guts and shook me again. 'You can stay here until you've calmed down and then maybe – maybe! – you can come down and have dinner with us.'

I continued to sob. Everything felt like I was doing something wrong. Perhaps Dad felt the same way too; it was just that neither of us could express it.

Primary school was an endless round of rules and regulations.

'Please may I go to the toilet?'

'No! You should have gone at break-time!'

'Yes, but I didn't need to go then!' (Also, I had developed an inability to urinate when I could hear other people's voices. It is a problem I still have now.)

There was the daily ritual of assembly each morning, itself packed full of rules. And everything was turned into a competition. Certificates were handed out to the class judged best at walking into assembly. A certificate was given to the class who had collected the most used postage stamps, which were then collected by a charity and – somehow – commuted into cash for guide dogs.

Special privileges were given to those deemed most responsible, including the role of overhead-projector monitors. These children were in charge of organising the see-through sheets that had the words to our daily hymns on them. When the time came for singing hymns, they would ceremoniously place the appropriate lyric sheet on top of the light box on the floor, which used an intricate system of mirrors to reflect the words outwards onto the screen hanging from the ceiling. I was so jealous of them having their own special job for everyone to see, and I secretly loved it when they sometimes put the acetate on the light box the wrong way round and suddenly we'd be trying to sing 'Lamp My In Oil Me Give'. backwards.

The most pompous of all the groups, though, was the one that got to sit at the back of the school hall, behind tall music stands during assembly. When the moment came to sing the hymn, they would grandly stand up and adjust their sheet music in preparation for their solemn duty: they were the recorder group. They were so full of themselves. How they loved to accompany the school hymns with their shrill descants. They looked so smug as they took their recorders out of the yellow velveteen socks they kept them in, screwing the three parts of them together and then blowing like they were about to pass out. One of the select few got to play a special recorder that was as big as a child and looked more like it belonged in a church pipe organ – it was the tenor recorder. That player really thought they were incredible, and I loathed them – how I wanted to have a purpose! A reason to feel like I belonged to something.

During this time, I was an avid fan of the BBC sitcom *Keeping Up Appearances*, the ongoing saga about a suburban middle-aged lady who was obsessed with snobbery and proving herself to the neighbours. As a ten-year-old, I would say the person I related to most of all in the whole world was probably the lead character, Hyacinth Bucket, and at times, I saw myself actually as the actress who played her, Patricia Routledge. An unusual role model, perhaps, and one which added to my sense of discord with the world, but she seemed to be exactly who I wanted to be. 'Patricia Routledge wouldn't have to go out into the playground at break time when it's raining!' 'Patricia Routledge wouldn't have to do a spelling test on a Friday morning!' I would imagine to myself.

I didn't like the teachers, and I didn't like the immature children at my school. I had nothing in common with them and, especially after the friend dumping, I felt like they certainly didn't understand me. I craved being with my mum and my nan in the back of my mum's Nissan Bluebird, running errands and maybe popping to the supermarket to buy a 'French stick', or sitting at the kitchen table with the kettle making its comforting whirring sound in the background, signalling that, yet again, tea was about to be made.

Almost every day I desperately attempted to convince the school secretary I should be sent home because I had a sore throat or an upset stomach – or on one occasion 'stomach cramps'. If this failed, then I was resigned to staying in this prison of a school for the rest of the day. Since my friends had dumped me I preferred to just play on my own, as that meant I didn't have to spend time with the other children so prone to screaming, making a mess and changing their mind about whether or not they liked me.

In fact, I didn't like playing at all really, as I always felt too embarrassed or too self-conscious about pretending and playing games. I was Patricia Routledge for goodness' sake! A version of Patricia Routledge stuck inside a child's life – I already understood the world and just needed to be treated as an adult – why did no one understand this?! I was ready to go out and get a job around other adults doing grown-up things like throwing tea parties or going on cruises.

If the friends I had chosen didn't want to know me and the other children irritated me, then I had only one option left for companionship during playtime: dinner ladies. Not the Victoria Wood sitcom, as it hadn't been written yet. 'Lunchtime Supervisors' is what they are now known as. Mrs Warwick was a key member of this team, and also she was a friend of my mum because she stood with Mum at the school gate. There was no way she wouldn't support me. Back then, collection from school at the end of the day was a much more straightforward affair – mums (and occasionally dads, especially the ones who had lost their jobs) waited just near the school gates, and once the teacher saw that the clock had reached half past three exactly, they would walk the class up to the edge of the gates and then set them free amongst the huddled mass. It was assumed that each child matched up with their correct parent – I don't know what happened if there was a spare child or spare parent at the end of all of it, as I always managed to find mine.

Mrs Warwick was to be my greatest ally during this turbulent time in the first few months of Year 6. When I had decided to make her my new friend she was talking to a much more formidable Glaswegian dinner lady but I waited for a pause in their chinwag and politely said hello and engaged them both in conversation about the weather. I felt like I was home; I didn't need my old so-called friends. I was ten years old and I could engage Anne Warwick in great chats about where was good to go on holiday and I felt like I was getting the adult conversation I so desperately craved. When I was feeling so alone and confused this dinner-lady friend proved to be my hero – my knight in shining armour.

At the start of one particular break-time, I was walking through a corridor to the playground when I discovered the doors were open on a large, untidy cupboard filled with design-and-technology equipment, namely small saws, screws, pieces of balsa wood and MDF along with hammers and mallets. It was all shoved in so haphazardly that the door wouldn't close at all. The equipment had been presumably purchased as advanced craft supplies for older children in the school to experiment in constructing things.

It was very exciting to me – though not the technology equipment per se. In the hands of another child, they would have found this equipment and decided to use it to make something wonderful to express themselves causing other people to be taken aback in awe. For me, though, the sight of an untidy storage space stirred an instinct deep within me and I was powerless to resist what my soul commanded me to do: tidy it. It was a mess! Bits of balsa wood were shoved carelessly on various shelves, as though the messy other children had used it and not bothered to tidy it away properly. Lo! How I disliked them! Not only did they not understand me or not want to be my friend, they were also so untidy – so thoughtless! Finally, I had a job – a calling! A purpose. I would be able to look those stuck-up recorder players and the overhead-projector monitors in the eye because I too had a role to perform!

I sorted the wood into the correct types and put each type into specific boxes. I sorted the screws and nails into their various sizes and found receptacles to put them in. I used scraps of paper and sticky-back plastic to label them, writing the labels with the calligraphy set I'd been bought the previous Christmas.

The whole thing was my secret project. What I enjoyed most was that it never seemed to end – there was always something more to be tidied or sorted or improved. If the teachers had found out about it, they would have sent me out to the playground to be on my own in the corner or to talk to the dinner ladies again. However, I rejoiced because here I was in my own organising paradise, a place of my very own that no one knew about. It was like my secret garden.

Occasionally, if I trusted someone enough, I would ask them to assist me. The few who did come and join me in my fantasy of order and labelling soon got bored of being bossed around. '*No!* That's not how to store the C-clamps! They should all be aligned around the same way . . . Oh, what's wrong with you? Give it to me! . . . I'll just do it.' The other children deemed this the very opposite of fun, and so I was relegated to stacking boxes of sandpaper on my own. But by being on my own, I was finally happy. Looking back, I realise it is hardly surprising that I didn't have a huge number of friends.

I should emphasise that no one had asked me to do this. It was in no way sanctioned by a teacher or some school technician. If anything, I had found a loophole in the system whereby I could get out of going into the playground for freezing-cold break-times. No one on the teaching staff even noticed me as they were having coffee in the staffroom, perhaps just pleased that *someone* was taking the trouble to tidy up their equipment. Perhaps, looking back, Mrs Warwick knew exactly what was happening and was only too pleased that I had found something to do with my break-times and left me to it. In any case, I was delighted not to have to mix with the other children and I was thrilled to have my own little empire that I could tidy and use my calligraphy pens on.

My halcyon days quietly tidying a school cupboard were not going to last forever, though. Perhaps there have been other things which I have found more daunting in a way, but nothing really compares to the feelings of dread I felt during Year 6 at the prospect of having to go to senior school. Leaving a school of four hundred children to go to a place where you are expected to cope alongside adolescents who were anywhere up to eighteen years of age shook me to my core. I would be a child (albeit a Patricia Routledge one), having to hold my own amongst dreaded teenagers.

I was terrified. Largely because of the rumours and titbits of information I had gleaned from the people around me. The older kids on my road talked about how their gym teachers had made them take showers after PE. The thought of it was harrowing. Surely you'd be able to get out of it?

'No!' they gleefully told me, 'Even if you just splash a bit of water behind your ears, get dressed and attempt to scarper, the teacher will always know, make you strip off and go back into the shower again!' I didn't show my bits to my own family, never mind a teacher and a class of boys I barely knew. They hadn't even bought me dinner! The idea of it seemed so undignified – why would the world treat me like this?

I was realising that my grandiose patrician deportment at the age of ten was starting to make me a figure of fun, and since I had no way of hiding it, I often embraced it so people would like me. My draconian teacher in Year 6 was a huge person who had short hair and wore long jumpers. She boomed at me when I was attempting to tap dance on the linoleum by the coat pegs – 'They won't have any of this at secondary school, you know! They'll shout "Jump!" and you'll shout, "How high?" – so you'd better buck up your ideas!'

Why this new school had to be so anti-everything, I couldn't understand. I imagined it was how conscripts feel at the start of a war, being forced into machismo institutions like the army against their will. I was becoming more and more anxious and found that atop everything else, I still wasn't great at making friends.

I think being an eccentric, sometimes very emotional, Patricia Routledge-obsessed loner, my parents had a sense that I needed to be toughened up in preparation for the next leap of going to secondary school and also for life itself. My dad made me watch two films. The first one was the mournful *Kes* – a story of a working-class boy with a horrible home life who befriends a kestrel which (*spoiler alert!*) gets killed by his brother, all set to a depressing folk flute soundtrack against the backdrop of the Yorkshire Moors. The only moment of comic levity is when the PE teacher forces Billy to have a freezing-cold shower after football. I think it was supposed to be comically grotesque, but it didn't make me laugh at all. If anything, it confirmed all of my darkest fears about what the children up the road had warned me.

The second was the film *Midnight Express* about a man who, seemingly on a whim, tries to smuggle hash out of Turkey, gets caught and sent to a Turkish prison with no hope of being released until (*spoiler alert!*) he escapes. It's a terrible prison where the inmates are routinely beaten and brutalised by the guards but then the main character starts doing yoga and then (*spoiler alert!*) seems to shag the other bloke in his cell. I never actually got to watch the end of the film, though, because my mum walked in just after the beatings scene and said, 'He can't watch this film – it's far too violent!' and switched it off, so in my mind, he did just stay in that prison forever. I've never tried to smuggle drugs, though, so I guess Dad's teaching must have worked.

What's more, there was talk of having to play rugby at secondary school, a game I had no idea about except that I was sure I wouldn't like it. I hated when I was made to be part of a group of boys at the best of times, never mind when they were throwing each other around in the mud. I might get claustrophobic in the scrum. A family friend's son had once demonstrated a rugby tackle on me and I had got winded – I couldn't breathe – and yet everyone around him thought it was hilarious, even though I was rolling around on the floor, casually asphyxiating.

The main thing I didn't like about being made to spend time with groups of boys was when, by default, we got addressed as 'lads'. I found it impertinent, even as a child, that I was being lumped in as one of the other boys, as though we were all the same. 'Hellooo!' I wanted to shout, 'I'm literally right here! I'm clearly not one of the lads, am I?! I'm Patricia Routledge!'

I was well into my thirties when I was told by a manager in Côte brasserie in Brighton, 'Sorry, lads, we're full tonight.' I was so annoyed I nearly slapped him round the face with my gloves.

It was a good job the rest of the male voice choir were there to hold me back.

My parents thought it would be a good idea to send me to Cubs, I think in a further bid to 'toughen me up' and make sure I wasn't totally surprised if I had to spend some of my time with other boys, in a PE lesson, for example.

We had a lovely Cub Scout leader – or Akela as she was technically known – and I would chat to her through the serving hatch of the Scout hall at the start of each meeting whilst she kept the register. Her bright face framed by huge glasses always seemed pleased to see me, and she was happy to indulge me in my chats, which, even though I was ten years old, were already erring on the side of 'middle-aged woman'. I would look forward to our discourse on the importance of good garden maintenance and also listing what I wanted to get for Christmas. It was all fine until she needed to deal with a mum who, annoyingly, had a question about something like falling into arrears with paying the subs, even though their family had a Range Rover. Akela would look apologetic and, to my mind, disappointed that we had been interrupted, but would say, 'All right, Tom, I'll just deal with this – why don't you have a kick about with the other lads?'

How could it have gone wrong so quickly? I thought she understood that I was actually a middle-aged woman from a sitcom trapped inside the body of a ten-year-old boy – how could she not realise I couldn't kick anything, never mind do it with the 'other lads'. I wasn't one of the lads myself, so how could I be around the 'other' ones? I stood at the side awkwardly, feeling misunderstood yet again, and waited for us to be told to get into a circle and salute the flag, something I was very adept at doing.

I attended Cubs every Thursday evening and can still see the Scout hut room now, with its faded herringbone parquet flooring, the white lines of an indoor tennis court over the top, glass doors with the wire cage running through the mottled glass, the smell of dust and the many flags denoting the various elements of the Cub Scout Group.

After Cubs, boys were eventually supposed to progress up to the older group, the Scouts. Scouts always looked like it was much more to do with preparing boys to be in the army but Cubs was more preoccupied with ceremonies that took place in a circle in the middle of the floor and then demonstrating a skill and collecting a badge. The ceremonies, in addition to saluting the raising of the flag, involved pledging allegiance to the Queen, promising to do my best and also squatting down on the floor to, again, promise to do my best, but this time in unison. I think the Lord's Prayer might have been thrown in for good measure.

I did promise to do my best, but it seemed like they weren't specific about what I should do my best at. I just assumed I hadn't found my field yet, and so continued being average at everything. I had about three badges, whereas most of the other boys seemed to have whole armfuls of them, which they proudly wore up their sleeves. Mine were in First Aid (I had to put another boy in the recovery position), Drama (I think I just got that for my everyday life) and then the Home Help badge. For Home Help, I had to help Mum with the hoovering and cleaning the bathroom and she had to sign a form to confirm it. I was already doing this anyway, and I knew I was definitely doing my best here. If they had ever questioned me, I could easily have described to them my work on the technology cupboard but they never queried it; I think they could see I would be very good at helping around the home.

I think I attempted to get one for rope tying but that was only because I really enjoyed looking at the wall hanging of various knots positioned by the door. I loved how it resembled a medieval tapestry, but seeing as I couldn't get my head around a sheet bend or a half hitch, I knew I was never going to make it.

Despite it being a vaguely militaristic experience, I much preferred the Cubs to the harsh world of Year 6 at school. I liked Cubs' rituals and the routine; somehow, once you were used to them, there was a lack of pressure. It felt like a rarefied midweek escape under the guidance of Akela and her trusted team of helpers.

During this first term of Year 6, it was still undecided which of the local comprehensive schools I should go to, and then I was told that I should sit the test for the local grammar school. For Mum and Dad, it meant an opportunity for social mobility. If I got in there, I would be much more likely to get a steady, sensible job where I wouldn't be subject to the whims of disloyal directors at a suburban car dealership.

Unfortunately, the test was incredibly difficult, and I was devastated that I couldn't get my head around the questions. They were full of things like non-verbal reasoning – 'non-verbal reasoning' sounded to me like when you didn't bother discussing your argument but instead engaged in a full-on fight. There were questions like: 'If three triangles are in a line which are then followed by a square, what would you expect the next shape to be?' I didn't have a clue, since I wasn't a robot who could communicate in shapes, nor was I an ancient Egyptian able to understand hieroglyphics instead of actual words. I was about to start crying because I was so frustrated, but the boy opposite me burst into tears first. I knew that on top of being frustrated, I didn't want to be unoriginal as well, so I did what I had got used to doing at this time and swallowed my feelings.

I failed the grammar school test. Things were going from bad to worse, as it was deemed that I was now at the age when I should leave the Cubs and join the Scouts. I would be saying goodbye to beloved Akela, whose chats I loved and who I noticed always cried when we had to do the Scout parade for Remembrance Sunday in the council car park.

Apparently, it was time for me to become a man, or at least a version of a man. Done were the days of me being a sixer (leader of six other boys), smartening their woggles and telling them to polish their shoes. I would now be a boy amongst men again and someone who himself would be told to smarten up his uniform. Growing up, the impending start of secondary school and the expectation to be a 'man' was advancing apace and I was not happy about it.

The activities weren't nearly as much fun as the ones Akela planned for us at Cubs, like making Easter cards with paper doilies. Instead, the Scouts were focused on the more masculine pursuits of hiking and lighting fires. There was to be a hike in the coming weeks and since I was too scared to go to any kind of camp (why travel to something you've already got in abundance?), this seemed much more manageable, and I said I'd be in attendance, just so it seemed like I was trying.

I checked with the leaders – for there were several now, all of them much less chatty – about what would be appropriate attire. Dress codes have always been a worry for me and I would hate to turn up unsuitably turned out. 'Hiking boots, waterproof jacket, warm clothes underneath!' barked the leader impatiently, as though she had lots of things to be getting on with.

'Ah well, now, that's great, super, in fact – only thing is, I haven't got hiking boots, but I have got wellies – will they do, hmm?' I said light-heartedly like I was back talking to Akela about my favourite biscuits.

'Absolutely no, it won't!' the young woman said and marched off. I was so upset, partly that I didn't have the right footwear but mainly because I really didn't like her tone. After all, I was only asking. It felt like adults kept on trying to make me feel like I was somehow ridiculous. I wanted to shout after her, 'We can't all be dressed like we're in *The Great Escape*, you know!' but my heart was in my chest, and what's more, I was scared of her.

The main activities for those early weeks consisted of being round the back of the Scout hut learning to make a fire. I was there with some boys, some of them as much as three years older than me. I was desperate not to seem like I was upset about the welly conversation and prove I was a fully fledged grown-up. Patricia Routledge would be able to cope, I was sure of it. I knew some of these other boys went to the comprehensive school I was to be going to, having failed the grammar school test so spectacularly.

'When you get to our school, Tom . . .' said someone I shall call Felix, one of the boys who would be described as 'tall for his age'.

'Yes?' I said, trying to sound confident but failing.

The tall boy continued, ' . . . we're going to beat you up.'

'Oh,' I replied. An awkward pause followed as I wasn't sure what the appropriate response would be. There wasn't much else I could say, though I wondered why they didn't just do it here and now if they were so desperate to beat me up. Perhaps because casually beating someone up wouldn't be part of the Scout code, even if they did do their best at it.

From my side of things, it was certainly a difficult conversation to conclude. I could hardly say, 'Right oh!' and then carry on.

If I had replied with something more defensive like, 'No, you won't, I'll beat *you* up!' it would have been met with gales of laughter, as clearly this wouldn't happen. Not with my posh voice and wellies instead of hiking boots.

In the car home that night, I told Mum. 'Oh.' She sighed. Another drama I had found myself at the centre of. I could understand – it was getting exhausting.

'Mum! You're not listening, they said they're going to beat me up when I start secondary school!'

'OK, but what do you want me to do?'

'I don't know! But you can't just say "OK".'

The following day, Mum was driving me and my brother back from school. It had been another busy day learning about the Industrial Revolution: coke smelting, the steam engine and the importance of Quakers in the eighteenth century. Year 6 was certainly a serious time. 'Felix's dad said he's going to speak to him. He's going to apologise.'

'*What?!*'

'After what you said – I told Dad, and he spoke to Felix's dad, who was very sorry to hear it and he's going to make sure Felix apologises.'

'Mum! What are you talking about? Why did you do this? You did it without even telling me. Oh my God, I am so embarrassed! I am going to look like such a baby! Like I can't even take a joke!'

'You wanted us to do something! When I told Dad, he phoned him straight away.'

'Oh God, this is terrible!'

'You were annoyed I wasn't doing anything.'

Suddenly, I was crying, gasping for breath between words as the tears were too much. 'How – am – I – supposed – to – start – secondary – school – if – everyone – thinks – I'm – a – baby?!'

'Speak to your dad when he gets in.'

'I am so angry at him! Why didn't he talk to me first?'

Dad only got home as I was getting into bed. I was so self-conscious about being a child, somehow aware of how young I was and so ashamed.

'Dad! Why did you do this without telling me?! I just didn't know what to do. You didn't have to speak to his dad. Now it looks like I can't fight my own battles.'

'Well, Tom, you can't. Clearly.'

'I know, but I don't want everyone to know that!'

'Look, I never had a dad to stick up for me, so I know I'm always going to stick up for you.'

The feeling of being looked after made me feel even more childish; it was a combination of feeling overwhelmed with love and an anger that I needed this protection, which somehow made me burst into tears all over again.

The following week's Scout meeting rolled around, and I tried not to think about it. 'Erm, did I say I was going to beat you up? I was only joking!' said Felix, sat on the floor round the side of the Scout hall with his mates. 'Jeez, can't you even take a joke? Haha, I'm sorry, OK? I'll make sure no one beats you up there, don't worry.'

I just wanted the moment to be over. I was still so embarrassed about the reality that I needed my dad to stick up for me. 'Haha, yeah, of course I knew you were joking! God, my dad gets so involved, doesn't he? Yeah, yeah, I knew that . . .'

'Sure,' he said, and then rolled his eyes before he carried on talking to his mates. The bonfire lit by the other Scouts was taking hold and smoke filled the air.

Despite my dad's protection, my world was changing rapidly and I didn't know what to make of it. If only I could have tidied it all up, put it in neatly labelled boxes and stacked them nicely in the cupboard, then I could have closed the door completely and been on my own. Finally away from the stress of other people, finally allowed to be just like every other normal ten-year-old and left to watch *Keeping Up Appearances* in peace.

'Do what YOU want to do, Tom — stop trying to do what you think other people want you to do!'

Whenever I asked for Dad's advice about doing something I wasn't sure about, this would be his usual retort. It always seemed so straightforward to him, yet for me, being co-dependent and a people-pleaser, life seemed so much more complicated.

4

We are Mom and Dad now

I've been to Japan. I don't like to mention it, but it's true, I have actually been to Japan. It's the sort of place, once you've been there, you can't stop talking about. Much to the tedium of those around you who like to remark sarcastically, 'Oh, you've been to Japan, have you? Really? You never mention it . . .' But, yes, it's true, I have actually been to Japan.

Dad's attitude to life was very much that we should grab it by the horns and do things. Or, as he would put it: 'Stop bloody worrying all the time – do what you want to do.' It's not the sort of mantra people would have framed as a poster, but maybe one day it will be.

At the time of going to Japan, I was living in Brixton in a flat with two friends, who were both in a couple. They both seemed more experienced at living like grown-ups than me with a sensible routine of shopping at the weekends, balanced evening meals when they got in from work and using hand cream before bed. I liked spending time with them but I knew I wasn't functioning as an adult as they were. I was twenty-nine and I had moved out of home for the second time. I moved out to live in North London when I was twenty-four but then I moved back home again when I was twenty-eight. I dreaded telling Mum that I was moving out again, so I told her over the phone when I was on the way

to a gig. It made sense, I explained, to be closer to town for getting to gigs – I needed to be on a Tube network! So glamorous.

I think my parents were confused by me feeling a need to live
away from them, but what they didn't understand – or what
I couldn't explain to them – is that you need to be away from
home to go on dates with people, especially if you want to invite
the date back, or worse, go back to theirs. One might assume that
going back to theirs would eradicate the problem – presuming
that my parents wouldn't be called upon for a lift there – but
when you have a mother who can't sleep until she's heard you
come in the front door, you are under obligation to always let
her know where you are if you don't come home. A flirtatious
evening culminating in a stumble into the hallway in an impas-
sioned embrace is somewhat derailed by an interruption such as,
'Hang on, I've just got to phone my mum to let her know what
I'm doing.'

'Are you going to tell her everything?'

'Oh no, I'm just going to tell her I'm staying over at Rob
Beckett's house again.'

'Aren't you worried that she'll just think you're in a relationship with Rob?'

'Oh no. And to be honest, if she did think that, she'd probably
be quite happy about it – she really likes him.'

'Don't you think she'd like me?'

' . . . '

My dad always wanted me to have the confidence to do what I
wanted to do in life, but how could I when I didn't know myself
well enough to know 'what' I wanted? I was getting more confident about writing stand-up material but I was still trying to
work out who I was on stage. Sometimes the audiences liked me,

sometimes they didn't and sometimes *I* didn't. If I talked about being gay, I worried that the straight audiences at gigs wouldn't understand because it wasn't their life. If I talked about mundane suburban things, people were confused by my posh accent. Fundamentally, I felt like I was still always trying to please other people.

In terms of furniture, my room in Brixton had, at first, just a naked overhead lightbulb dangling from the middle of the ceiling and a table by the window. I'd moved in with only a suitcase, because I didn't want to put Mum and Dad out by asking them to move my stuff, so I had brought only bare essentials with me on the train to my room, which looked like a boarding house from the 1930s until my flatmates bought me some flowers.

I found a routine whilst living there and started to feel vaguely adult. I would leave for gigs before my flatmates got home, arrive back after they'd gone to bed and wake up after they'd left for work. I didn't see anyone except for the other comics and maybe a train conductor. If my parents had seen it, they'd have been heartbroken. 'Why would you want to live there when we've worked so hard to make a lovely home for you?' It felt so hard to explain to them that I felt like this was what you were supposed to do when you are a young adult living in a city. I imagined the looks on their faces, and it felt like a heavy price to pay for other people's opinions and the dream of an occasional fumble on a stairway landing.

One of the reasons I had wanted to be closer to town was so that I could be closer to gigs. I had adopted the policy of saying yes to every gig I was offered. One of Dad's mottos was 'If you're not earning, you're spending' and so with limited income I knew that I had to err on the side of earning. I also knew if I allowed myself the time and space to think, 'Well, do I want to travel two hundred miles by train when snow is forecast to do a twenty-minute gig for a student union?' I would probably say no. But if I didn't think about it and always said yes, then I would always be busy, and more than that, I would be earning and I would be proving myself. I never asked my parents for money and I paid them rent when I lived at home, so I wanted to be able to show them that now I could pay for myself in the big wide world.

I always knew I would have to provide for myself and that I had to live within my means. It was one of the reasons I didn't go to university – I didn't know how I'd pay for it on my own and I didn't want to ask Dad for the money. I think this is a factor for a lot of teenagers that people don't realise: if you don't know anyone in your family who studied for a degree, you have no idea how it will be funded and you're often too embarrassed to ask.

My dad had another motto of 'If you want something done, ask a busy person', which I had translated as the busier you are, the more things you will be able to achieve. If you spend time thinking, nothing gets done, except maybe more thoughts about why you shouldn't do stuff. Busyness begets business.

The year was 2012, and the Olympics were coming to London. Everyone was moaning about how the Tube network would be closed and people were being discouraged from going into London during August in case it was too overcrowded. There was outrage over a rumour suggesting the government was placing a rocket launcher on the roof of a block of flats opposite the stadium in case there was a terrorist attack. Everyone was moaning about the cost of all these new stadia. No one seemed to want the Olympics. But I had a sneaking suspicion that once it started, people might change their tune.

However, making myself do any gig offered to me meant I could save a bit of money and, since I'd been advised not to take a show to the Edinburgh Fringe in the summer – 'The thing is, you're not new enough for people to be excited and you're not famous enough for people to come' – I decided I wanted to use the spare time to go somewhere. I had never gone travelling when I left school. Friends of mine had gone to places like Thailand and Cambodia on their gap years and in their university summer holidays. Since I didn't go to university, there was no gap and no summer holiday to act as a space for me to fling a backpack on and flounce off to see the world. I felt so inadequate compared to those people who travelled, as though I could never be as cool as those intrepid backpackers and explorers of my generation. Instead, I had always wanted to go to work to make my fortune in showbiz. Ten years later, and I was uneducated and not making any kind of fortune in showbiz, so I decided I may as well do something for my own pleasure – I would stop trying to earn money and allow myself some time to spend some money. What's more, an adventure might be just the thing to teach me something about myself.

Looking at Virgin's website, the cheapest place to run away to in August seemed to be Japan. I was delighted as I'd always heard how expensive it was, but this seemed well within my means! What I had not realised was that it isn't getting there that is expensive, it's everything *once you get there* that costs cold, hard cash. Also, no one would leave their city when the Olympics were on, surely? But everyone had been telling me how terrible it was going to be and how they already hated it, so I assumed it was going to be simply awful.

'Japan? Why do you want to go there?' asked Mum, confused and with great anguish. My parents have never been particularly big fans of travel. My mum has always loved beach holidays, but I think my dad found them difficult to justify, an indulgence perhaps, when time could be better spent working to provide better security for your family, for your future.

'Who will you go with?'

'I'll go on my own. Everyone will be busy.'

The truth was, I hadn't asked anyone because I was too scared they'd say no and then I'd feel stupid. Or worse, if they said yes, I might end up having to do what they wanted, and I just wanted time to do whatever *I* wanted! It absolutely made sense that I would have two weeks on my own to discover the world.

Landing in Tokyo, I boarded the famous metro system, blurry-eyed and dizzy from jet lag, and immediately started to see the famous Japanese politeness in action. A prominent sign proclaimed, *You may be having fun, but please, keep your voices down* and underneath, to really bring the matter home, *Please be careful of the volume of your voice on the train.* I realised that, finally, I was home! A place where people took manners as seriously as I did! I was suddenly desperate to fit in like I really belonged.

In August, Tokyo is intensely hot, which explained the cheap flights. It is humid and subtropical beyond belief, and because it is a huge, concrete, highly populated city, it was perhaps the hottest place I had ever been to. Owing to the fact that I always travel in a blazer – flying through the sky feels like a special privilege, so I always make sure I look my best as a mark of respect to people – I was sweating profusely. And because I couldn't understand the signs and the maps in Japanese, it took me half an hour to find my way out of the station.

I was so hot, but, knowing that I couldn't check into my youth hostel until the afternoon, I took myself to look at a temple. It feels like the sort of thing you should do in Japan; go and look at all the beautiful temples that seem to be everywhere. It is perhaps the equivalent of arriving in Britain and deciding that you must go and look at all the churches. Yes, they are very beautiful, but unless you are an expert in stained-glass windows or hold a particular longing for brass rubbing, they can get a bit repetitive.

Politeness is prized above all else in Japan, and I quickly realised my Western manners seemed oafish by comparison. I was unsure of when to bow and when to remove shoes, where to walk and what to say to the people exclaiming in chorus, '*Ohayo gozaimasu!*' each time you walk into a shop.

Everything is ceremonial, which I would usually enjoy, but since I didn't know what everything meant, it felt absolutely terrifying and so overwhelming. It must be how people felt when I invited them round for dinner.

I walked through a long, elaborate walkway and through a red gateway garlanded with lanterns. In the long approach to the temple, there was a courtyard with people holding long wooden tubes to shake solemnly at small wooden boxes around the walls, which I presumed was in tribute to the dead, but it was too difficult to know. I realised why people use the services of a tour guide so they can ask questions like: 'Is it impolite to enter the temple while someone prays to their dead ancestors?'

My fear was quickly allayed as I approached the temple, because a sign strewn across the entrance in typically polite fashion stated, *Please. Don't come in.*

I often think about that sign and wish I had one at home.

I'd booked into a youth hostel, because that was what my friends had done on their gap years.

Overheated and overtired, I found the hostel up an alleyway in a residential street; the houses dripped with plants – green foliage everywhere. Youth hostels are designed to be easy for young people to hop into. They are casual places, relaxed and fun, and instantly I knew I didn't like them. A rack for removed shoes was crammed by the doorway, and it reminded me of the bouncy-castle parties I'd been to as a child – shoes shoved to one side in excitement at the thought of bouncing. This felt considerably less exciting, and the aroma felt somewhat reminiscent of a gym changing room – quite out of kilter with the immaculateness of everywhere else in Japan.

Being a bit older, I'd looked for hostels with single rooms. In terms of my booking, I realised something had been lost in translation when I discovered the 'single room' was in fact more of a single 'space'. That is to say, it was a plywood cupboard with a mattress in it. An ingenious space-saving solution and a streamlined design, yes, but combined with the exhausting heat, the long flight and my bedroom situation, I immediately wanted to arrange a flight back home. Mum was right – I should have stayed where I knew where everything was. In a room full of these fitted coffins, mine was midway along on the second row, meaning I had to climb a ladder to get into it. As a very nervous child who preferred the comforts of home, I had never been to sleepovers, so the novelty of bunk beds had never been explored with me. More than that, I was just ever so slightly too old to be staying in a youth hostel.

I crawled into my human-shelving-unit-cum-coffin for a nap and owing to jet lag, slept until the following day. I woke up early and remembered that the Olympic opening ceremony back home would be on the television. I sprang out of my wall-coffin like an energised Dracula who was also somehow in a bunk bed and went to find the television room. It was crammed with the younger people from the hostel, people from around the world, excited to see what this Olympic games would hold. The whole of London looked magnificent: David Beckham was like James Bond on a speed boat, there was a huge theatrical performance showing the Industrial Revolution and the invention of the internet, the Queen jumped out of a helicopter. It was amazing, and everyone was screaming with delight.

'You're from London?' asked the Dutch woman next to me, perplexed. 'Why aren't you there?'

It felt ridiculous to admit I was still hellbent on following other people's opinions when I responded, 'Oh, everyone said to me it was going to be shit.'

Travelling alone has many benefits, but it does mean spending a lot of time in your own thoughts, and as ever, my inner monologue tends to be quite critical. It's like carrying round a *Daily Mail* journalist who criticises the way I sit or how I must look to other people. I always have a terrible fear that people must be thinking, 'Why is he travelling on his own, anyway? He must be a serial killer. Probably on the run from the police.' It is thought patterns like this which probably explain why I find it quite difficult to relax and why I tend to like being busy with less time to think. Plus, of course, I am a serial killer.

With the youth hostel being so warm it could be described as positively clammy, I knew that the most refreshing thing I could do was go to one of Japan's famous *onsen*. Onsen are basically public baths often filled with spring water, and like everything in Japan they are resplendent with customs and rules. The first one being: clothes off. Everyone has to go completely naked – anything worn outside is considered totally unclean. I was not prepared for this at all, as I thought that in Japan things would be formal and ceremonial and therefore very much buttoned-up. Nudity was something I have always been terrified of.

I was given two small towels, a flannel, a kimono and a bar of soap in a basket. In our Western society, we get so het up about clothing. For a society underpinned with formality and manners, it might seem strange that nudity is considered completely fine, but I think it reflects more on the West's pre-occupation with sex and the assumption that as soon as flesh is on show it must mean sex is about to happen. It's like we still live in Victorian times when an ankle could be considered lurid and in some households table legs had to be covered in case they turned everyone on. As one nurse friend of mine says, 'After a while, elbows and arse-holes – they're all the same really,' which did make me question whether he has any medical training at all, as I don't know if this is completely true.

On entering the onsen, I had to strip and then bravely walk to the pre-bath cleansing area. The idea of getting straight into the water like we do with hot tubs in places like Orpington would be regarded as totally disgusting by people in Japan. Luckily, I seemed to be the only one there, which pleased me, though it then dawned on me there was no one to watch to see if I was doing it right. Admittedly, the idea of sitting there gawping at a Japanese man while he cleans himself might not be totally polite either.

Small stools were provided at each washing station. I sat at one and began to do my best to shower and wondered why sitting down seemed preferable. As I began my process of starting at the top and working my way down (isn't that what everyone does?) I was feeling very smug, like I had lived in Japan my whole life. A man arrived and walked to his washing station. He shot me a horrified look. That was when I realised my first terrible error: the small flannel wasn't for washing, it was for sitting on at the onsen washing station. I must have looked so appalling.

It being the middle of the day on a weekday, we were the only people there, so there was no way I hadn't been noticed. Freeing in a sense, as I had already messed up, I had much less awkwardness walking over to the onsen itself completely naked. It's exactly the same feeling of walking across your bathroom at home apart from being totally public. I had to remind myself it wasn't really like a public place; it wasn't as though I was walking across a shopping centre. I was expecting a shop assistant to come up to me to say, 'Excuse me, sir, I'm sorry to bother you, but do you realise you are naked?' like in one of my many anxiety dreams. However, it is actually quite a refreshing feeling, especially considering how humid the city was.

It was considerably less refreshing when I clambered into the large bath itself and realised it was actually burning hot. Literally like a bath. Heated as it came up from the hot springs. Too embarrassed to get out, I sat there in the water, just me and the Japanese man; me squirming in the heat and him looking on at me, disgusted.

I was a *gaijin* – the Japanese word for 'foreigner'.

It had been said to me beforehand that you can only experience something for the first time once. Japan is a perfect example of this because it is so different to Europe. I felt I should love it but just didn't know how to participate. Bowing is almost a constant greeting throughout the day. That may sound straightforward, but at times, there are different sorts of bows. For example, sometimes the bowing is much lower down, to show added respect, whilst eye contact during the bow is regarded as downright impertinent. In fact, many Japanese people discourage gaijin from bowing, as getting it wrong is worse than not doing it at all.

Uttering *'sumimasen'* was the thing I did most of. It means 'sorry' and also 'thank you' and also 'excuse me'. It was particularly handy, as I felt like I was committing constant faux pas almost as soon as I woke up.

Despite its heat, the youth hostel proved to be a good place to hang out of an evening. One night, the other residents were playing Jenga at one of the tables in the bar area there. I sat at the bar and ordered a drink. A translation book was casually placed on the table and felt like it had been put there by the owners, sensing I was struggling to fit in. Flicking through, it did seem to have some strange options for what the authors thought a tourist might need (these are the actual translations from the book, so please don't write to me if they don't make sense). Chat-up lines like:

'O-shiri no katachi ga kakkoii yo' – *Gosh – what a good-looking hip you got there!*

'Zenshin ga urekitta kajitsu no yoo da' – *Your body is just like matured fruits!*

These particular lines made me wonder if my approach to relationships had been so bad after all. The book went on to recommend phrases like:

'Kon'ya wa moetsuki tain da' – *Burn me down tonight.*

Which really sounded much more like something that needed an ointment. And warnings like:

'Tenchoo ni shiretara taihen yo' – *It will be a big problem if the master finds us.*

Suggesting that an amorous encounter in Japan can really take a turn. Especially as the phrase book concluded with:

'Boku-tachi mo oya ni nattan da ne' – *We are Mom and Dad now.*

It had been a long-held ambition of mine to travel on the bullet train, and so travelling to Kyoto had an added excitement. The whole design is like a duck-billed platypus, and boarding it had the feel of a futuristic space station with its sleek sliding doors, silently opening alongside the gently curved windows. The seating was immaculate and even though it was a few decades old by that point, it had been cared for to such a high level that it looked brand new. It was like boarding a spacious aeroplane.

The carriage was almost empty, though it felt strange to refer to something so futuristic with the arcane epithet 'carriage'. The only other passengers were sitting across the aisle from me: a lady in traditional Japanese clothing and make-up sat next to her husband, who was wearing a more Western-style suit. She treated him like he was incapacitated, though he clearly wasn't, tucking a napkin around his shirt before serving him his lunch by hand. How intense it seemed as she spooned soup to his mouth. She pored over him like a mother in a fairy tale might with a baby. At the end, he stood up and walked to the toilet.

The train conductor asked to see tickets, and I gave him mine with a smile. Once he was happy with our passes, he moved to the front of the carriage, and before pressing the button to open the sliding door, he did a low bow to us, which seemed very reverential and quite out of kilter with my previous experiences on Virgin Trains' London-to-Manchester route.

Kyoto is a much prettier city than Tokyo, full of traditional buildings and smaller garlands of lanterns. The sort of thing you would find in someone's imagination if you asked them to picture Japan. The equivalent in England would be something equally picturesque, like how American people sometimes imagine that we all live in a thatched cottage near a castle. They seldom imagine Purley Way in Croydon.

It was a relief to check into somewhere else to sleep. This time, it was a more traditional space with tatami mats to sleep on. The Japanese attitude to rest and peacefulness is very well thought out. The lighting along the corridors is floor-level and dimmed to amber, glowing through basket-weave shades. Doors are sliding panels made of paper. Everything is thought about with such care that I lament how appalling it must be to Japanese people that Westerners go through their days with such little consideration of how best to live your life.

I had believed I would be totally self-sufficient on this trip and not need to speak to anyone else. However, when Geoff came trundling in, I was very much relieved. Geoff was a built man a couple of years younger than me with dark floppy hair, walking boots and shorts, with a backpack and wheelie case and a travel pillow round his neck and baseball cap in one hand. He was from Reading, and clearly more of a bloke than I was. He was the sort of person I would never normally make friends with at home, but it occurred to me, perhaps this is what travel really is – travelling far away from yourself to try on different personality traits and different friendships. Since no one knows us we can try being different in a way that our self-conscious selves at home wouldn't allow for fear that someone might say, 'What are you doing, talking like that?' or 'He's an unusual friend for you, isn't he?'

I decided that I should be a bit more blokey in order to make this friend. 'All right?' I said to him chummily, bowling over to shake his hand. 'I'm Tom.' I didn't even know if he spoke English at this point, but on an instinctive level, I felt like he did have a look about him that suggested he was like me and had a diet of mainly bread.

'Oh, hello!' he responded. 'I'm Geoff.' Annoyingly, he wasn't nearly as blokey as I had decided he was, and actually, he was a bit posh. I imagined he probably went to a public school and worked in finance.

'How you finding Japan?' I asked.

'Hot!' he said, laughing and wiping his brow with his travel pillow as he removed it.

'Wanna come see Kyoto?' I said, still trying to be a character from *Only Fools and Horses*.

'Yes, absolutely! Let's go! Immediately.' Wow, he was keen. But after several days of ambling round places at my own lethargic pace, this was welcome. 'I really want to see the bamboo forest!'

'Absolutely!' I said, resorting back to my posh voice, which he hadn't heard before, so it probably sounded like I was making fun of his use of 'absolutely'.

We took the train to the nearest station, and then he said, 'Oh great, a taxi!' I had decided beforehand that taxis were off limits, as they are so expensive in Japan, but Geoff was much more direct and much more keen to just do things, regardless of the expense. Also, I was delighted to finally travel in some comfort.

Japanese taxis are a whole ceremony in themselves. The doors are self-opening, so there is no need to touch anything.

Upon entering them, the futuristic style that Japan is famous for disappears, and instead you find yourself sitting in a small compartment filled entirely with lace. It is like you are travelling in your very own doily, as though somehow you have been scooped up and carried along in the Queen Mother's petticoat.

We arrived at the bamboo forest as the sun was starting to set. It is exactly as it sounds: a forest full of bamboo trees. We walked through it feeling tiny in comparison to the tall green shoots towering over us. The trees went on and on into the distance, enveloping us in their emerald eternity, like when mirrors are placed opposite one another and you can see forever. It was really quite mesmerising.

Geoff punctured the silence. 'Very popular with people committing suicide, this forest.' I didn't think it was that bad. He then boldly asked, 'Do you want to come and see some Japanese theatre?'

'Sure,' I replied, always open to new experiences.

We stopped for a photograph, with the endless bamboo trees trailing off into the infinite distance, and then sidled off to get another frilly taxi back to the city.

Noh theatre is usually performed in the round with the actors wearing traditional Japanese clothing. Nowhere in Kyoto would be more apt to host this than the district known as Gion, a maze of old buildings bedecked with screens and shutters, a place where you might even see a traditional geisha flitting between meetings. Walking through it after dark, lanterns lit our path as Geoff led us to where he was sure we would find the Noh theatre. On arriving at his co-ordinates, though, there was nothing, just a crossroads. We walked on to see if there was a sign or any indicator at all but ended up walking through the maze of alleyways and tiny streets to come back on ourselves and ended up in the same place.

'It's around here somewhere, I just know it!' said Geoff, seeming frustrated and agitated, sweat building up on his forehead in the evening humidity as his determination intensified. Wearing his heavy walking boots with shorts, he started to resemble a Scout leader, with me his solo Scout. If I was honest, I didn't want to go and watch any traditional Japanese Noh theatre, but I knew that the alternative was another evening of not doing anything cultural and probably just falling asleep.

'Let me see the map,' I proffered, trying to help. ' . . . Well, it looks like it should be here. But this is just a wall. Maybe it's wrong on the map. Let's walk along here to see if it's nearby.' We walked down a narrow lane, no more than an alleyway really, and suddenly a well-lit structure presented itself. Like all the buildings, it was one storey high with up-lit cornices and sculptures giving it a grandeur the neighbouring buildings didn't have. This was obviously the theatre.

We strutted up the well-lit pathway to the front door. Sliding open the screen door, we walked through to find ourselves surrounded by ornate paper screens and ornately carved pillars holding the structure together. It was beautiful. Confusingly, unlike theatres I had been to in London, there were no posters advertising forthcoming performances, no kiosk from which to buy a ticket or pick up a pamphlet, no box office employee to ask about tickets. And so we tramped further across the mats, Geoff's boots making them squeak underfoot, and journeyed into the building further to find more discreet rooms, empty and dark, hidden behind paper-thin screens. Feeling even more confused, we seemed to be lost yet again.

Finally, a woman appeared from the dark corners, dressed in a very traditional beautiful red kimono, her face immaculate in its make-up and her hair huge and glossy. She stopped in front of us and just as we were about to ask her what time the show started, she looked us up and down and bellowed, 'This is my house!'

We were horrified. We had committed the ultimate social crime of not only wandering freely around someone else's home, but doing it whilst also wearing our dirty outdoor shoes. We felt disgusted at ourselves and immediately attempted to bow and say '*Sumimasen!*' as we hurried out.

There would be no Noh theatre that night. Though part of me wondered if we hadn't just found ourselves in some sort of experiential-based theatrical moment. Instead, Geoff and I went to have dinner and think about what we had done.

Back in our shared room, Geoff didn't seem to acknowledge the thoughtfulness of the Japanese resting ritual and immediately put on the big overhead light and turned the perfect sleeping arrangement into a brightly lit paper box. I subtly turned it off, but because I had done it subtly, he thought there was a fault, so went back to switching it on again. It felt like it had all the restfulness of my local ASDA on a Saturday morning. I started to wonder if Geoff was a perfect travel companion after all. In the morning, in a further disregard for restfulness, he woke me up early to say goodbye.

I journeyed on to Hiroshima on the bullet train. Overall, Geoff had been a fun companion to see Kyoto with but I was glad to be back on my own. Whenever I am with someone else, I find myself trying to please them by agreeing to go along with their plans. I think for that reason, I am probably quite susceptible to joining a gang, as I think I'd just end up agreeing with whatever they wanted me to do, like spray painting an old lady's shed, just to avoid the social awkwardness.

Arriving in Hiroshima, I made sure I was staying in a hotel room which definitely had basic things like a floor and a bed to get out of. The small modern capsule rooms felt like utter luxury, complete with a bed, pyjamas, hanging rail and chair. It wasn't ensuite, but each floor did have an onsen, so over I went to attempt the ritual that I had failed at before. I was confronted with a Westerner who was using the space to do some yoga stretches. When you don't have any clothes on, this really is a speedy way to get to know someone, and certainly very different to my acquaintances in England.

'Hello! I'm Rob,' he said, his face between his ankles.

'Oh, hello, I'm Tom.'

'How's your trip?'

'Oh, great, thank you – so much to, erm, see!'

'I know, right? What a place. Probably my favourite place I've been to so far.'

'Oh, you've been travelling around a lot then?'

'Yeah, about two and a half years.' I immediately wondered, ' . . . But how?' A two-week trip away from home was stressful enough for me, but for some people, a few years was completely fine. I couldn't understand it – how did you pack enough pants? How did he feel about not having a job and not doing anything constructive with his time?

I quickly realised that Rob didn't worry about things like that, as he never stopped talking. 'I used to be an electrician – well, I wasn't qualified as one, but I just did it anyway . . .'

'Oh right? Is that sensible?' I knew the answer anyway, which was convenient as he continued talking.

'I lived outside Exeter for a while – always missed the train, though, so I used to just walk home – took me three and a half hours.' He never seemed to stop his asinine chatter. I could barely keep up. ' . . . The French are horrible . . . The moon landing was a hoax, definitely . . . Everything worth inventing has already been invented . . . No adventures are possible, as everything worthwhile has already been experienced . . . I slept with a prostitute in Thailand but she didn't want paying . . .'

A stronger person than me would have just said good night and left the onsen and Rob for the night and forever more. I am not that strong, and instead found myself unable to get away from him. Perhaps it was tiredness, or perhaps it was fear of what he might say if I just left – the social awkwardness would surely be too great – which led me to making mindless conversation as we both sat there naked. 'Where is your favourite place you've been to?' I asked politely, not caring about the answer.

'Laos! Definitely Laos. In Laos, right, you do this thing called tunnelling. It's amazing.'

'Oh right, what is—'

'Tunnelling in Laos' – he kept repeating the word 'Laos' for some reason – 'what you do, yeah?'

'Yeah?'

' . . . is you sit on, like, a tyre and then you go down the river on it, and all these bars, right, they sell you drinks, so you just get really pissed as you go further down the river and then you just, like, sit in a café watching cartoons till you fall asleep. Laos is amazing, you know?'

'Gosh, that does sound amazing,' I said, lying.

I couldn't get rid of Rob. He followed me back to my cabin room and asked me what I did for a living. When he found out I was a comedian, he couldn't wait to bombard me with questions.

'Do you get heckled?'

'Sometimes.'

'I love Jimmy Carr.'

'Oh right.'

'Hey, maybe one day you'll write a routine about me, eh?'

The next morning, he still wouldn't leave me alone. How I wished I had learnt to say, 'I'm going to have a day to myself today, but thanks.' Dad would have said, 'Do what you want to do!' but that's easier said than done with someone like Rob. With someone like Rob, he required a different sort of Dad-phrase like: 'Bollocks to you, I want to be on my own!' but I just haven't got the sort of voice for a phrase like that.

Instead, I found myself on a bike, cycling in the unimaginable heat around Hiroshima. The humidity was described as 100 per cent, which to my mind suggested we were swimming in a river. Clothes were immediately drenched with sweat.

Rob seemed to have boundless energy, which was unsurprising, considering he hadn't had a job for the last two and a half years. He was relentless in cycling up steep hills, and I was too embarrassed to say I was too tired to keep up. How I missed Geoff.

I asked a Japanese man to take a photograph of me on my bike – I wanted to prove to people at home that I had exerted myself to the point of sweating. I gave him my camera. Luckily, he seemed pleased to practise his English with me and then took the photo.

It can make you feel self-conscious to ask for a photo of yourself, though. This was exacerbated when the man looked at the photograph and grimaced. 'Oh,' he said politely, 'maybe just one more.' Clearly, the first one had been hideous.

Rob and I went to the peace garden and museum in the centre of Hiroshima, which commemorates the atomic bomb dropped over the city in 1945. The dome is the only building that still stands – the tiles and brickwork almost completely destroyed, leaving a skeleton standing in proud defiance. The museum explained in horrifying detail what damage the bomb did to the city and its people. For people around the world, the image of the mushroom cloud forming above the city is what we think of. The experience for the many people in Hiroshima was just a flash of light, like a photograph being taken, and then nothing but a shadow left burned onto the pavement.

It was a solemn moment on a trip that had been otherwise so busy and so frantic. In amongst the hushed reflections on war and human suffering, Rob marched up to my side and loudly declared that he was hungry. 'I'm starving! Come on, let's go for ramen.'

In the punctured quiet after he spoke I finally understood myself well enough to know what I definitely wanted, more than anything else: I wanted to go anywhere but some restaurant with Rob; I wanted to say goodbye to him and never see him or anyone like him ever again. I wanted to do this trip as I had set out to do it – on my own terms. At last, I felt like the trip had taught me to listen to Dad's advice and genuinely do what I wanted to do, not what other people wanted me to do (though in truth, I probably didn't need to travel all the way to Japan to learn this from Rob; I could have probably met a similar person on a bus in Sidcup). The trouble was, as ever, Rob didn't stop talking for long enough for me to tell him, so over dinner I watched him slurp his noodles with hatred, whilst he told me more about Laos.

'Next to Elton John I'm a pauper, but next to a pauper I'm Elton John'

Dad would often say this to reassure us he was happy with his lot in life, and that material wealth is always relative. I seem to remember him saying this at a barbecue and I was taken aback as I had never imagined he would ever compare himself to Elton John. Dad would never wear glasses like that, for example, and I don't think he ever met Kiki Dee.

5

We've had a lovely day and we hope you have too

Dad always knew what to do in every situation and he was very keen for us to learn good behaviour from him. Perhaps it was to show that it didn't matter what your background was, you could always show respect to the people around you, no matter who they were, and that was always a good way to approach life.

I learned to click my fingers in the New Forest. I was nine years old, and it was, at that point, the greatest achievement of my life. I had tried and tried to master it, but to no avail. My parents could do it, musical acts on television could do it, but again and again I found I could not.

We were staying in a 'nice' hotel. Dad was always adamant that we behaved ourselves in anywhere he referred to as a 'nice' place. It was a byword for the more blatant term 'posh', but I think to him 'posh' suggested something over the top in its fanciness, something that we wouldn't be part of. Despite growing up as a working-class Londoner, he was keen to show that even if you were from a modest background, there was no reason why you shouldn't know how to behave around other people. Hence the adage: 'Manners don't cost anything' – or as Dad would put it if he wanted to make fun of people who talked just like him: 'Manners don't cost nuffink.'

We were sat in the hotel dining room having breakfast. Perhaps somewhat bored, or at least distracted, I was trying, yet again, to click my fingers. After a lifetime of rubbing the tip of two soft fingers together to desperately try and make a sound, it finally happened and a short, sharp click emerged. I was elated. At last, I could be like the grown-ups around me! I hated not being able to do something. 'Look, Dad!' I said, clicking in front of my face in wonderment, clicking in front of his face, clicking my fingers over my head and from side to side like a flamenco dancer trapped inside a small boy, still in Year 5.

As the waiter walked past, I was keen to show him too and clicked abundantly to show him, and my dad lurched over the table and put his hand over mine, like a game of rock, paper, scissors, to cover my clicking digits.

Incidentally, rock, paper, scissors is a game which has never made sense to me, as scissors will cut paper, and a stone will break scissors, but when has a piece of paper ever stopped a stone? If this were the case, landslides could be prevented by producing a pad of writing paper, a biblical stoning averted with a papyrus sheet and coastal erosion solved with a box of envelopes and a Post-it note.

On this occasion, Dad's hand did stop this stone from rolling away down the hill. Looking me dead straight in the eye, in that voice that parents use that is both whispered and shouted, he urged, '*Never* click your fingers in a restaurant.'

I was devastated that my newfound skill had been immediately met with disapproval. This was surely a prodigious new talent and something that could set me up for life – perhaps as a cast member in the musical *Chicago* or as a Peggy Lee impersonator, specialising in 'Fever'?

'*Why* though, Dad?'

'Because it looks like you're clicking at the waiter to demand his attention – and that is *very* rude.'

'But I didn't do it to be rude to the waiter! I just did it to show my new skill!'

'Yes, but he doesn't know that, does he?'

'But I really like the waiter. He's got a bow tie! I love bow ties – I'd never do anything to upset him!'

'Just don't do it, please – we can click our fingers when we get outside.'

When we get outside? That didn't sound like a sensible answer at all. What a lot we would seem, stepping out of the hotel, all of us clicking our fingers like a family re-enactment of *West Side Story*.

It made me realise that behaving nicely towards people was important to Dad. To him, it felt like it was part of a contract that if he treated you nicely, you'd treat him nicely, and the world would be a better place to live. In a world of cruelty and unkindness, the least you can do is try and break the cycle in your own small daily interactions. It also reflected Dad's background of growing up with nothing – you might not be able to offer much to others, but you could still offer other people respect.

He was practical and straightforward, and I think, though he always supported me, he found my eagerness to lay the table like we were in *Downton Abbey* somewhat frustrating after a day driving coaches around London. My tendency to overcomplicate things could drive him to distraction. Yet despite this, we were similar in our ways: we were determined and sure that we understood the best way to do things.

'What *are* you doing?' he would call after me just as we were leaving for a day trip to a National Trust stately home – a day trip I had planned because I wanted to get ideas on how I might lay the Christmas table in our open-plan dining room. I had dashed back upstairs to make sure I had unplugged my Tiffany lamp and to double check that I hadn't left out any of my diaries. Diaries which contained hints to my secret crushes or the other boys at school I wanted to see doing gymnastics. It was unbearable to think that anyone might find these. Though, looking back, it was just another example of me overthinking and overcomplicating my life. Especially because the whole family would be out on the day trip together, so it would only be an unusually nosy burglar who declined to steal our video player in favour of perusing a closeted teenager's diaries about the boy at school he liked who played the clarinet and who I imagined would be very talented on the pommel horse and the uneven bars.

The National Trust visit involved driving to a big old house down in Kent. I think I loved the idea of wandering around the rooms of aristocrats, the chambers all leading into one another through joining doors. Huge beds and massive tables filled my heart with a sense that maybe we could recreate this in our terraced house built in the 1960s. I imagined myself parading through these long corridors and galleries, perhaps stopping to admire a photograph or sit in one of the chairs to admire the view. My fantasy was ruined by the presence of other people also coming to look at the rooms and the people working for the National Trust, wearing a tabard and advising people on the provenance of the wall hangings. I was prevented from sitting down in any of the chairs by thistles placed on their stately cushions, presumably to spike anyone who dared to place their posterior upon them.

Somehow, to me, these grand homes represented a refined way of living, a time when people knew how to behave with grace and dignity (whatever that means), and that ways of behaving were strictly codified. I longed to be part of it.

The slow parading through these rooms and reading of signs explaining the paintings came to an end and then the best parts of the trip could be embraced: namely the gift shop and the café. The gift shop sold a wonderful array of potpourri, greetings cards and waxed reusable shopping bags. Nearer to the counter were the more expensive broaches and scarves – scarves that you could wear over your head to look like the late Queen. CDs of Gregorian chanting, rulers, rubbers and biros were placed in the middle, mainly for children to buy on a school trip. For me, though, I didn't want to buy anything, other than the house itself. Since it was not for sale and I did not have any money, we went to the café instead and bought scones and sat in the window to admire the view.

Even at this age, I had a sense that I had to hold on to these moments when we were all together. As we got up to leave, Dad went over to another family sat by the door. 'We've had a lovely day and we hope you have too!' It was an unusual thing to say, but it was as though he wanted to say, 'We can all be nice to each other – it doesn't cost anything.'

The family smiled and nodded. 'Thank you, yes, we have.'

Dad lived stridently and directly in everything that he did. 'Do what you want to do! Stop worrying about what other people might be thinking!' was his constant mantra to me. He cared about behaving properly and treating other people as you would like to be treated yourself.

★

I'm old-fashioned. I don't like loud music and I don't like people being selfish. The reason I put both of these together is that I especially don't like people being selfish by playing loud music. I went to Tenerife and a Dutch family sat next to me on the beach and set up speakers. Actual speakers. The daughter started choosing songs from her phone to blast out for their family and thus everyone sat nearby.

Adding insult to injury was that she skipped just before the end of songs, and then, when trying to find the next 'tune' to play, she would play the introduction of songs before skipping the track and moving on to the next one. I am no DJ, but even I know it is a cardinal sin not to play to the end, even when choosing music in the car.

Imagine if everyone turned up with their own speakers and their own choice of music. It would be pretty selfish of me to turn up on the beach and start blasting everyone with my favourite Stephen Sondheim songs now, wouldn't it?

The mother of the family sat with her white smock and long white hair, her massive gold sunglasses perched on her nose as she surveyed the ocean's magnificence, clearly thinking, 'This was all fine and good, but then we came along and played our Ibiza chill-out CD and now it is *perfect*.' The father wore a small trilby, as though he was a playful character from a 1950s film about a cheeky man on a trip to Hawaii, which irritated me. He clearly wasn't any of these things.

I got up to leave, which was no mean feat, as I like to bring a lot of options to the beach to nibble on and so therefore had lots of things to gather up. I could have left the snacks behind on the beach but I hate litter, something which is also very selfish in my book (a phrase I use here quite literally). The mother smiled at me kindly in a way that implied, 'Pretty cool, right?'

99

and the co-dependent part of me was delighted. She almost had me smiling back, saying something positive like, 'Cool tunes!' to somehow try to impress or make friends with them. Luckily, I stopped myself just in time. I should have given them a piece of my mind but I was still too worried what they might think of me if I made my feelings plain – and what if people nearby saw and thought badly of me?!

So, I did the next best thing and glowered back and stomped off with my backpack on, towel rolled up under my arm, baseball cap on my head, tote bag I got free with a copy of the *New Yorker* full of fruits in one hand and a selection of still and sparkling water in a bag for life in the other.

The act of stomping off on a beach is made troublesome by the fact that the sand absorbs your feet with every step, so combined with not having enough hands to tighten my espadrilles on my feet, my stomping looked more like a snooty otter with his nose in the air while his lower half angrily dragged behind, slipping into the sand with every step.

It was a pathetic protest, especially as the family didn't even notice. Dad would have just said, 'Do you mind turning that down?' in a way that would have been upfront but not aggressive and shaming of them, and they probably would have obliged. I had a lot to learn.

Dad was direct, yes, and at times couldn't be stopped. However, this directness wasn't always well placed. At the age of fifteen, I was very keen on the library. One day, we had to return my rentals to Bromley Central Library or I would get fined for being late. The idea of being in trouble with the library, or anyone, worried me deeply. The three-week period that I had borrowed the Noël Coward song book and the video of the film *Mary Poppins* for felt like it came round so quickly. It was late in the evening when I remembered and I dashed downstairs apologetic and ashamed that I had forgotten, yet again.

'It's so late! Can't it wait until tomorrow?' my mum exclaimed, exasperated at my strange routine of borrowing song books to learn to play music-hall numbers from the twenties and thirties on the piano, as well as films set in the Edwardian period. I used them to escape into my fantasy world of music and stories – in my mind, the early twentieth century was a time when drama and theatricality were a staple of the everyday, and yet a time when people still had space to listen to a winsome melody.

'I'll take him,' Dad said. 'He can drop them through the letter box round the back – they let you do that.'

As ever, Dad gave me a lift like a dutiful chauffeur who doubled as my parent. He drove me into Bromley and parked in the car park opposite the Salvation Army. It was the easiest place to leave the car, as there was an alleyway between it and the entrance to the library. Dad was always pleased to find the easiest ways of doing things. I think he craved a quiet life, one where he could sit quietly and fall asleep in front of the television, and he was often perplexed at how I managed to add so many layers of concern about everything.

With the books under my arm, we started to walk along the dim alleyway behind the shops, making our way to the modern precinct and the library. We marched past old wooden pallets used for transferring stock into the shops, large bins holding flattened cardboard boxes and bubble wrap, and up ahead, a lonely discarded shopping trolley. As we walked on, I was alarmed to see a pair of legs lying on the ground ahead. At first I thought they were a discarded mannequin, its face, I imagined, still in dignified repose despite now lying destitute at the side of an alley. Only now the legs were more visible, the toes pointed heavenward, and yet as we drew closer still, to my horror, I realised that the mannequin was moving. It had come to life and was even making the sound of some distress. It dawned on me that it couldn't have been a mannequin but someone in great pain who needed rescuing – my young mind, steeped in dramatic story-telling from all those Agatha Christie books I also kept taking out of the library, assumed we had stumbled upon the victim of an attempted murder.

My dad strode on and didn't notice the impending Agatha Christie novel we were about to enter. As we continued on apace, the moans of the murder victim seemed to be getting more intense, the grey jeans and square loafers shuddering, presumably in terrible pain. I adjusted the heavy library books under my arms.

I could see through the cage-like metal bars of the abandoned shopping trolley to the murder victim on the other side. The chain hung from the trolley's coin holder on the handlebar, dangling ominously. The person who left it there clearly wasn't worried about losing their money, unlike me, who was desperate to avoid just a library fine of something in the region of forty-five pence.

To my terror, I saw that the murder victim was not recovering from the attempted murder but was, instead, in the process of still being murdered. A woman sat astride the poor man as he desperately tried to sit up, seemingly to push her away to save himself. Still, she seemed to be trying to do her worst, her head occasionally lurching back to exhale some sort of demonic laugh – all in all, it was a terrible sight to behold. My whole being filled with a peculiar feeling of wanting to help but also being intrigued to watch.

It was then that I realised they were on the floor by the bins, having sex.

In my prudish teenage way, this was much more horrifying than a murder. I was disgusted, yet still very curious about what was actually happening. My dad, impervious to anything but his own task of returning library books, marched onwards.

'Dad!' I whispered desperately, pulling him back by the arm – something I rarely did. 'Dad! We can't walk up here!'

'What?' he said, confused as to why the task couldn't be completed in the way he deemed most direct.

'Dad, we can't go up here – we'll have to go round!'

'What on earth are you talking about?'

'Dad! There are two people there having . . . *sex!* On the floor!'

'What? Where?' He sounded disbelieving, almost incredulous at this point. The lustful pair were barely fifteen feet away, a sad shopping trolley the only curtain between us and them.

'Oh, don't be so silly, Tom.' How was I 'being silly' when this was clearly a socially horrifying situation way too complicated for me to understand? The term 'silly' made me feel immediately ashamed for gauging the situation wrong again – as though 'concern' was on a volume control that I had yet to understand how to use properly. I felt like I had, yet again, failed to understand what was worth worrying about and what was not.

To my horror, Dad strode on ahead, defiant of anyone using the public byway after dark for their own nefarious deeds. Dad was never prudish – he was a Londoner and, as ever, direct and no nonsense – and so walked directly past the couple.

'Evening!' he chimed as he marched past the murderous-looking lustful tryst. I scampered along behind him, trying hard to avert my eyes and look at the wall but still helplessly glancing down to my right. They carried on regardless, themselves determined Londoners also focused on the task in hand, so to speak.

Heart racing in my chest and my face flush with embarrassment like a Victorian lady, I placed the books in the letter box specially designed for late-night book returning, and then as we turned to head back on our treacherous journey, I as ever had to go back to check I had delivered the books properly. What I was checking was never quite certain – I think I had a sense that I would return them wrongly and somehow be punished. I went back to push the letter box open to make doubly sure that the books hadn't become lodged somehow outside of the drop box and weren't exposed for any passer-by to steal.

'What *are* you doing?' Dad said, confused again by how I was taking longer than I needed to. I was indignant that I was the person accused of behaving strangely in this situation.

We walked, strident as ever, back towards the car. 'Dad, shall we go the long way round?' I pleaded, to spare the embarrassment of all concerned, though to be honest, it seemed that I was the only person who felt awkward about it.

'Don't be silly, Tom!' and we marched on, my heart ready to be appalled again by the terrible scene we were about to see for the second time. Dad strode on ahead again as I concentrated on the wall on the other side of the alley. As we continued, my senses heightened in anticipation of seeing the couple again.

I was almost disappointed to find the alleyway completely empty. The moment between them was presumably over, and they had both gone their separate ways home. The shopping trolley had gone too, as though they realised they should probably claim their pound, presumably their second one of the evening.

Maintaining the fine line between needing to behave properly whilst still being mindful that there are some people who choose to have sex on the floor of an alley by some bins has been a fraught path for me, and I often take blending in too far.

One of the part-time coach drivers Dad worked with doubled up as a member of the army who, as part of his duties, was also a musician. He was trained as a military medic and could also play the trumpet. Quite a combination of skills when you think about it and I hope he never got his shifts confused – no one needs a stretcher bearer blasting the injured with 'What a Wonderful World'.

He was blowing his trumpet – quite literally; not just shout-ing about his own achievements – at Trooping the Colour at Horse Guards Parade when I was sixteen. If you are not aware of it, it is the annual birthday parade of soldiers and their flag ('Colour') on the official birthday of the monarch. This trum-pet-blowing driver gave Dad two tickets, and Dad wondered if I fancied going. Of course, nothing could have thrilled me more. This was exactly the sort of thing I fancied going to.

More than that, the Queen's official birthday usually hap-pens on the second Saturday in June, and since I was born on 14th June, on certain years I shared my actual birthday with the Queen. Incidentally, I share my birthday with Alan Carr, Boy George and Paul O'Grady, rendering that title 'Queen's Official Birthday' more than a little apt.

I was desperate to be immersed in something as fancy as this, where the actual Queen would be right there, and surely her very presence would ensure everyone was on their very best behaviour. Already my penchant for dressing up, fanci-ness and superiority was stirring deep within me. I loved that we would be attending something where it would feel like it was Victorian times, chock full of ceremony and formal-ity, and at last we would be admitted to it. It felt like all my dreams had come true and I would be where I had always felt I belonged.

On one of my Saturday afternoons avoiding dogging couples in Bromley Central Library, I had done extensive research to find out exactly how the ceremony would work. I knew that standing up and removing your hat whenever the 'Colour' paraded past was a big part of proceedings and I did not want us to lose out. I also learned it is never called 'Trooping *of* the Colour', although I still don't know why. All I knew was that I liked rules, and I liked knowing boring things that marked me out to other people as special.

Getting organised to go out the door on the morning of the ceremony, my dad was taken aback when I came rushing down the stairs, on time for once, and carrying with me two bowler hats that I'd bought with my previous year's birthday money in a charity shop in Beckenham High Street. 'Dad, look, I got you one as well!'

Knowing that he couldn't disappoint me on my birthday, he managed to keep himself from recoiling in horror at something so out of fashion. My mum looked on, laughing, and my dad dutifully, though somewhat begrudgingly, put the bowler hat snugly on his head. My enormous head was too big for my hat, so it had to rest on the top of my crown. Leaving Charing Cross Station, we must have looked like the advert for the Bradford & Bingley Building Society, walking up to Horse Guards.

It turned out we weren't in a position to do much partaking in the traditions of the ceremony, as on arrival we saw where the tickets actually were. We wouldn't be standing up and sitting down when the flag paraded past, because we didn't actually have seats. We were standing behind a small rope fence on the gravel, below the posh people sitting in the raised seating behind us.

It did mean we got to see everything quite close up, including the horses and, appropriately for us groundlings, the horse shit. The posh people behind us in their military dress and morning coats stood and sat a safe distance from the muck, their feathered hats and tails quivering in the June sunshine.

At last I had my wish and turned back the clock, and it felt truly like I was alive in a bygone era full of formality and class-based ceremony, and in a cruel twist, my social class had been honoured perhaps too authentically. In days gone by, this is exactly where we would be stood – between the posh people and the horse shit.

My dad had gone along with it, though, and I realise now that, whilst I was trying to figure out how to behave and how to understand the complexities of my dad, he was also trying to figure out how to understand and fit in with me.

The Queen went past solemnly in her carriage; everyone cheered happily and no one clicked their fingers, or played loud chill-out music, or decided to have sex on the floor as she went by. I wonder if she saw us. Probably not. But if she had, I wonder what she would have thought of the two of us. 'Oh,' she might have thought with a smile, 'one does love Laurel and Hardy.' These two strange characters from the suburbs: my dad trying to watch his workmate in a solemn military parade without drawing too much attention to himself, and his son trying to turn it into a full-scale rendition of the musical *Mary Poppins*.

'Honour thy Father and thy Mother'

— Exodus 20:12

Dad took me to church on Sundays up until I was about ten. It wasn't the sort of church that taught the Ten Commandments adamantly, but I think I got the sense that I should be a boy who respected the wisdom of his parents.

Dad was inclined to impart somewhat more prosaic, perhaps less biblical, wisdom, thus:

'There's a difference between scratching your arse and tearing the skin.'

. . . A reminder that you don't always have to go over the top to experience life to the full.

6

Mary Poppins taught me it is rude to stare

A lot of my experiences as a gay man have felt like going out into the wilderness completely alone, either through shame or through not being able to make friends with people in the same boat as me (I suspect one led to the other). On these odysseys, I often felt completely terrified but something kept me going. Growing up, being gay felt so outside of the world I saw around me; I felt every step I took towards being out and 'proud' was turning my back on my parents, my friends and my background. The way I seemed to flee the safe, protective embrace of suburban family life felt almost like a betrayal, and for what? Just to try to find a world out there that might be accepting of my eccentricities and flamboyances, where I could fancy guys freely? That these two worlds could exist in harmony was beyond my reckoning at this point. I felt torn between a loyalty to my parents and everything they had done to protect me from the world – and the sense, as Dad would say, that 'We're not here for a long time, we're here for a good time.' I had to enjoy myself! On certain days, one would win out and then I would feel terrible remorse at not honouring the other.

When I first came out, if I went to a gay bar, I was often on my own, as most of my friends were straight. It felt too much to ask them to come with me while I tried to talk to people, tried to find a 'boyfriend' or essentially anyone to spend a date, a week or just the night with. It would be too much to ask my straight friends to sit there passively with no options for themselves as I desperately tried (and failed) to even make eye contact with someone.

Going to a bar on one's own felt brave and like a bold statement – a step towards meeting other gays, like they did in the TV show *Queer as Folk*. However, in most gay bars loud music and flashing lights meant talking to someone, or anyone, was nigh-on impossible, and it felt exposing being alone, as though people might be staring at me pityingly. This made me feel so ashamed (though at the same time I was furious that no one was staring). Everyone else seemed to be there in groups of friends or on dates themselves, so it wouldn't make any sense for them to start talking to me. The truth was, at this point in my life, in my twenties, I had no idea how it was done. By 'it' I mean all of it – I didn't know how to make new friends, how to talk to new people, chat people up, ask someone out on a date, never mind sleep with them or start a friendship or, God forbid, an actual 'relationship' (which according to all the films and all the songs is the main aim of everyone's life).

Standing awkwardly in the corner of a bar with no friends or dates, the selection of free magazines stuffed in the racks by the door was a godsend. With their aid, I could look like I wasn't just there to desperately meet a new friend-boyfriend; I could, in fact, pretend I had just casually popped into this loud bar playing Gwen Stefani videos around the walls to catch up on the day's news, albeit very specific gay news.

I was sure popping in to cafés and bars to sit and read was something people did in continental Europe all the time. The film *Amélie*, my favourite at the time, was basically all about a

Parisian café where single people just popped in for a coffee or a glass of wine to be around people while reading periodicals detailing the day's events. I dreamed of living a carefree French experience, even though I had only done French to GCSE, so could only talk about my last family holiday and the historical sights. Sadly, Soho in London in the mid-2000s was definitely not Montmartre in Paris. However, I did my best and perused these magazines, feigning great interest in them so that no one would suspect that I didn't know what I was supposed to do in these bars.

These 'periodicals' carried a selection of horoscopes and articles about subjects as scintillating as gonorrhoea (once referred to as 'The Clap', though I can't imagine anyone contracting it and wanting to offer a round of applause). The fact that I still confused this sexually transmitted infection with the name of the narrowboats people use to get around Venice perhaps gives some indication as to how little I understood.

The magazines would also include articles about various club nights that had taken place the previous weekend, replete with photos of either big hairy men wearing harnesses (bears), smiling in the corner of bars decorated with open brickwork and neon lights, or confident younger gays with their tops removed to show off their defined chests and spikey haircuts in clubs in Manchester with TVs on in the background, probably playing the latest Kylie video (the one constant in our turbulent lives).

In the back of the magazine were adverts for penises. I assumed they had people attached to them but you seldom saw that. Largely, they were photos of men's groins with a phone number. I don't know if the penis itself picked up the phone when you rang – I can't tell you as I never called. Perhaps no one called, in which case they must have had very disappointing evenings sat limply by the telephone table in the hall.

In the mid-2000s, the back pages also included phone lines where you could hear about the various exploits of young men. Each phone line was titled with a flavour of what to expect: 'My local remand officer gives me the punishment I deserve . . . round by the bins!' Everything seemed to happen round by the bins. 'Can't believe my football coach took me round by the bins and showed me his massive whopper.' I don't know how they avoided being sued by Burger King.

In essence, they were pre-recorded monologues of various sexual adventures. In many ways, the equivalent of a Radio 4 afternoon play but with more fisting and mentions of council estates and sportswear. And of course, bins. 'And now on Radio Four, The Lady in the Van by the Bins Sees a Fisting', the announcer would say. It was a very simplified depiction of *EastEnders*-like characters, caricatures of what the phone-line owners presumably dreamed 'normal men' might be like, whatever that means. These fantasised 'normal' men had adventures where their normalcy was subverted in an endless round of surprising sexual activities.

To make these hyper-masculine subversions even more fantastical, the monologues were all performed by actors, and the adventures that their characters went on were as ridiculous as they were sexual. I once met someone who performed them for a bit of extra money and he flamboyantly explained (a credit to his acting abilities) how they'd had to use a watermelon and a hammer to recreate the sound of sexual squelching – thus revealing that however 'macho' these characters might be portrayed as to the outside world, we are still fruits.

In the magazine, other club nights were advertised that seemed to take place in a railway arch somewhere. Patrons were encouraged to dress up in football kits, or high-vis jackets and construction workers' uniforms, or even just in tracksuit 'trackie' bottoms and T-shirts to meet other men attracted to this kind of thing. Ultimately, it made me think that everyone else in the gay world must be going to these sorts of events all the time, and, I imagined, must be having endless amounts of sex. It confirmed how removed I felt from these notions of traditional masculinity, much more inclined, as I was, to reel off a Gladys Cooper film quote or a Noël Coward lyric. As a result, I must be totally unattractive and unwanted and maybe I should just take my polished brogues and self-tied bow tie and sit at home, never to trouble anyone in the community, because surely I would never meet any other people who were like me.

Of course now, in the wake of *RuPaul's Drag Race* and the celebration of the ballroom scene of New York from the mid- to late twentieth century, all of this dressing-up and these club nights could be seen in a very different light. That is to say, drag. The 'masculine realness' or 'construction-worker realness' is as playful and creative as any drag performer that ever walked a ballroom in London or New York City. If only I had known! If only these performers had taken themselves less seriously! I needn't have felt so terrified after all.

In among this charcuterie platter of gay magazines were also adverts for something referred to as 'saunas'. These were different to the infrared variety that celebrities put in their spare rooms nowadays and were far removed from the sophisticated Scandi-navian log cabins in the Swedish countryside. Rather, these were thinly disguised sex clubs, or 'bath houses' as they were referred to in America.

More confident and brazen friends of mine had been to them lots of times. They would occasionally talk about them and afterwards, as they walked away, I would hear straight people whisper, 'Surely, they can't be legal?' as though something so downright hedonistic must be against the law.

The adverts were usually torsos of Adonis-like men, or cartoons with bubbles rising up to decorate the sauna's opening hours. The idea of them terrified me. It was exactly the sort of place I knew a person could catch gonorrhoea, and what if everyone there took drugs? When I was seven years old, my dad made me swear that I would never, ever take drugs. It was a strange thing to make someone in Year 3 do. I wasn't even allowed Coca-Cola, never mind cocaine. I dutifully swore, though, which meant I couldn't turn my back on him.

I had always thought of myself as a nice boy. My parents and their friends had always said so. I was polite and made conversation at neighbourhood barbecues. I had been head boy at my school and instigated that our school lay a wreath at the local war memorial on Remembrance Sunday, and everyone said what a dignified gesture it was. My parents were so proud of me for being popular, though this was mainly with my teachers. My homework assignments had always been done on time and to the best of my ability. I never, ever wanted to let them down by going off the rails into a spiral of sex and drugs on a gondola.

However, despite being exhausted trying to maintain this 'nice boy' persona, by the time I had reached my mid-twenties, I was starting to think I might want to have some sort of relationship. The advice 'You're not here for a long time, you're here for a good time' kept ringing in my ears and making me panic that time was running out. I had to get on with wearing builders' clothes and taking my top off in bars. My life was ticking away! I didn't want to get it wrong or look back with regrets.

I had read all the guides to gay life available, namely books by people like Alan Hollinghurst, whose characters couldn't seem to leave the end of their road without shagging someone behind a bush. Since these were the only guides available to me, I was convinced that by not living like those characters, I was falling behind in my homework assignment and failing the exam of adulthood.

I could never pluck up the courage to enter one of these saunas. Each time I would scurry past, stealing a glimpse of what was contained therein, and then go back to looking at scented candles in the window of the gift boutique next door.

Returning home, I would be frustrated and angry at myself for not having the courage to be like all the other gays. My dad would cheerfully ask, 'Everything all right?'

I'd put on a smile and say, 'Yeah, Dad,' and change the subject.

Then, on the night of my twenty-second birthday, I went out for a couple of drinks. I was relatively drunk, but not too drunk. At the time, I felt so old. Saying good night to my friends, I pretended to go home, but I was determined to finally experience what this whole world was about. No longer would the cautious, family-obsessed voice in my head triumph and keep me prisoner in the world of 'No, Don't!'

I battled the voice inside telling me it was late and I was tired, so maybe I should just head back home where Mum and Dad might be waiting up for me. The voice in my head taunted me: 'Everyone else goes to these places – you've seen it in those magazines you picked up for free in the noisy gay bar. They wouldn't lie, would they? What's wrong with you? Why are you such a coward? Haven't you even got the courage to experience life? When are you going to finally live rather than spending all your time at home with your parents like a stupid child?' As you can tell, my inner monologue has always been very encouraging. I ignored all the things I had been taught about not walking through dark car parks and wandering around unknown areas of London at night and went up to the door.

The building looked like an office or warehouse closed up for the night with only the amber glow of the reception desk inside to guide me in. A buzzer had to be rung to gain access, and standing in front of the glass door waiting to be admitted, I could see my reflection. In my face, I saw those of my mum and my dad staring back at me, confused as to why their nice son would be in a place like this. There is nothing wrong with gay saunas, of course; they are not illegal and there is nothing wrong with anyone using them. However, in my small suburban way, they felt so removed from what I was used to, and thus forbidden (but also so intriguing), that I concluded they must be something I should fear. Immediately, I started to think about my family life and its homeliness: the television on in the background at all times, my dad making a whistling sound through his teeth to let everyone know he was home from work, my mum roasting potatoes and blow-drying her hair almost constantly, though never at the same time. 'What are you doing here in a place like this? Shouldn't you be looking for love – not sex?' I could hear them saying. In truth, I don't think I knew the difference and to be fair to my parents, I doubt they'd even have such strong opinions. The spirit of my mother followed me in through the door, not to stand in moral judgement but to stand in judgement of the decor.

The aggressive buzzing sound from the door being unlocked woke me up from this internal tussle. It was the signal that the experience had begun. Opening the door, I realised it was heavier than I expected, and so I really had to drag it open, clumsily, getting one shoulder inside to lever it open like an insect crawling my way in. I approached the counter, a small opening in a wall, resembling the serving hatch in my grandmother's assisted-living flat, and I paid the admission with cash, because I didn't want this visit to be traceable if I paid using my John Lewis credit card.

'All right, love?' said the older man behind the serving hatch brightly in a Mancunian accent despite not really having any front teeth. 'Here's a towel – do you know where you're going?'

'Actually, no, I—'

He could tell I was nervous. 'Just through the double doors – changing room on the right, and then there's signs everywhere else. Condoms and lube in every room, OK?' He smiled and planted two thin towels in my hands, a coloured rubber wristband popped on top like a cherry on a cake. It was the same sort of wristband they used to give Dad at West Wickham Swimming Baths to denote how long you could stay in the water, many years before places like the glamorous Pavilion Leisure Centre opened meaning there were many more places available to swim. 'All the red arm bands come in now!' the lifeguard would holler.

The man had to then buzz me through the double doors to the changing room itself, which made it feel like a prison. In a way, the changing room was also like the swimming pool, but it didn't have the screech of people having fun in the water just round the corner. Nor did it have the smell of chlorine, which to my childish nostrils was a signal that we were going swimming and a precursor to the best possible time.

The bench in the middle, complete with coat hooks above, reminded me of the changing rooms for PE at school and all the fettered curiosity they entailed; the memory of the chlorine smell now replaced with that of Lynx Africa as worn by the other boys in my year. How I had spent my teenage years trying to keep a lid on my lustful teenage thoughts about them! The

changing room was edged with slightly bashed blue metal lockers framed with grey surrounds, and the strip lighting overhead
created an atmosphere of cold functionality. 'Strip lighting' was
exactly what it was.

A man in his forties was getting changed after his swim in
these mysterious waters. As he put his work clothes back on,
he looked just like a million people I had seen on the trains and
Tubes that day. My overactive imagination immediately jumped
to assuming he came here because he was trapped in a loveless
heterosexual relationship that he couldn't possibly get out of –
his wife explaining to the kids that again, 'Dad's got to work late
tonight.' In my mind, they nodded and solemnly dipped their
chips in their ketchup, knowing their dad was lying again. His
wife choosing the word 'work' and avoiding the word 'job' for
obvious reasons.

Clumsily, I entered the space, trying to stay close to the locker
allocated on the key on the rubber band. Having changed, I then
attempted to pack up my things and stumble back to the locker
wearing nothing more than a towel and carrying with me the
clothing of the day. I am not body confident at the best of times,
so this was very much an unseemly dance, and the tortured office
man glanced over before offering a friendly, 'You all right, babe?'

'Oh yes, all good, thank you!'

His calm self-confidence suggested that he probably wasn't in
some tortured straight relationship at all and that the only person
being tortured was me with my overactive imagination.

As it was the mid-2000s, some khaki cargo trousers, a clashing
T-shirt and a pair of Converse trainers was my outfit du jour.
This was a time when I tried to dress according to what people
in those gay magazines seemed to wear. I was desperate not to
stand out because, at this point, people were very much not into

flamboyant or eccentric-dressing twenty-somethings. Homo-phobia was rife, not just on the streets, and no longer confined to the straight community. Now it was sometimes from the other gays, who, through a sense of shame and fear, I suppose, had turned on themselves, resenting their sexuality so much that they resented anyone who had the audacity to even seem gay. Dating apps were full of people looking for 'masculine' or 'straight-act-ing' men: 'If I wanted someone feminine, I'd be straight.' It was deeply hurtful to any of us reading them to think that after years of struggling to finally be ourselves, we would then be met with another layer of disdain from our fellow gays who didn't like us for who we were.

The people with this attitude were potentially the victims of circumstance, perhaps brought up under Section 28, when being gay couldn't even be mentioned to young people, and who, in the absence of role models, had no one to teach them better. I often wonder how things might have been different had so many of our role models not been taken by AIDS.

These 'masc for masc' angry gays had currency, because some-times it seems to work that if people are horrible to us, sadly we can end up being even more enthralled with them. And so these judgemental gays, with a very rigorous set of values on how peo-ple should behave, seemed to have pervaded not just dating apps but also a lot of my thoughts about myself.

It was this voice that was in my head in that locker room and when I went out into the rest of the sauna. I tried to walk in a way that these imagined people would perceive as apparently masculine – presumably without moving my hips at all and standing with my shoulders back and my chest pushed out. As someone who had never been near a gym, I had no definition to my chest so what I was pushing out was really just some ribs and a couple of nipples.

This ridiculous attempt to walk in a certain way sadly didn't disguise the fact that I had a voice that basically made me sound like Noël Coward doing an impersonation of Kenneth Williams. I knew I shouldn't speak if I wanted to keep up any kind of 'masc' act. This was difficult, as I knew, body confident or not, my only way to endear myself to someone would be to talk to them because the only thing I am good at is inane chatter. The reckless side of me wanted to do the absolute opposite of what I felt I should do – I suddenly had an urge to do a Mae West impersonation by putting my hand on my hip, leaning against a wall and asking a passer-by to 'Come up and see me sometime.' I didn't, though, as I was too scared.

The sauna was set out like a sort of Roman temple, but strangely it also had carpet. Perhaps the oddest area was the café bar furnished with chesterfield sofas that wouldn't have looked out of place in my aunt's house in Australia – she'd saved up for one for her fiftieth birthday because its olde-worlde aesthetic went with her collection of bar mirrors and copper kettles, which reminded her of England. This place didn't seem very olde worlde, although it did have the smell of old smoke and a selection of soft drinks and KitKats. More and more, this whole adventure reminded me of those swimming baths in West Wickham.

A slight-built older man was working behind the snack bar – or tuck shop as it seemed – selling filter coffee and Monster Munch while a couple of men, one in his sixties and one in his thirties, wearing nothing but towels, watched the television monitors on either side of the counter. At this point, the television was showing a late repeat of *Emmerdale* and it seemed like the Dingles were having a much more entertaining time than these guys.

I wondered if this was the sort of place I could make a connection. I didn't really have a plan for what I wanted to happen explicitly. I think I had a hope, tragically I suppose, that I might meet someone.

I bought a Sprite and went to place myself on a chesterfield opposite a younger guy who seemed about the same age as me. Sitting in a towel on a shiny faux-leather couch is fraught with problems, though. On making contact with the seat, I immediately slid forward on the fabric. The action of sliding down like this immediately made an unfortunate flatulent sound against the sofa and people turned round to look. I had almost come off the edge and nearly found myself on the floor. My confidence felt like it might be about to ebb again.

The voice in my head returned. 'God, you're so pathetic you can't even make conversation with anyone – why have you even brought yourself here? What are you doing with your life?'

'All right?!' I exclaimed at the man opposite me, thinking maybe he would be in the same frame of mind, looking for a friend in this strangely anonymous place.

He looked up in confusion. I felt like my 'All right?!' greeting was too enthusiastic and too keen, and he might walk off in disgust that I was even attempting to talk to him.

'Ello, arr yoo OK?' he said in a French accent. He wasn't being aloof – he was just French! Much more understandable. This was becoming more and more like *Amélie* by the moment.

'Yes, thank you. Are you French?' I said excitedly.

'Yes, I amm frum Toulousse.'

I couldn't help myself; despite not being qualified, I jumped straight in. '*Est-ce que vous avez une bonne nuit?*' was my bizarrely convoluted way of asking him if he was having a good night.

'You know,' he said, 'we are sitting in a gay sauna with nothing more than a towel on – you don't need to use such formal French. I think "*tu*" would be better than "*vous*", *non?*' he said with a wink.

I smiled, embarrassed. I had got ahead of myself. He downed the last of his can of Coke, stood up and walked off.

Part of me felt humiliated. A boy in a man's world. I had no business being there among the real guys, the gay men who knew what they wanted and went to a place like this to get it. They weren't afraid of the world and overthinking things all the time. They just seemed to be able to go out there and get it. Or at least that was the way they seemed; I never really got to talk to them.

A room beyond the café had a small swimming pool and a hot tub with white plastic sun beds round the side where men seemed to be asleep. The small swimming-pool room led into a corridor with a steam room and sauna next to one another. The smell of damp was overwhelming, probably explained by the corridor opening up into the carpeted floor of a stairwell, presumably having absorbed years of steam. The whole thing seemed like an odd combination of a sex club and a photocopy shop.

The stairs led to a vestibule and the beginning of a dark, narrow corridor lined with small doors. The small rooms had small beds in them, like Goldilocks might have found at the beginning of her tour of the three bears' house. There were more than three bears here, though. I felt immediately alarmed at what might happen in these rooms. Obviously, I realised it was sex, but in my mind I wondered if it was something more sinister, like torture or some sort of medical experiments. Both of which I have since learnt are sexually very exciting for some people. Here, the harsh utilitarian strip lighting gave way to a much more sedate ambience. A festoon of LED lights had been clumsily arranged high up on the wall, as though we were in Santa's grotto at Christmas. Some of the more bearish, older clientele certainly resembled Santa, albeit Santa dressed just in a towel, like he might have come back from the pool or perhaps taken to sporting a sarong on his summer holiday.

The festive corridor looped round a central block of rooms, so people seemed to be circling endlessly but not getting anywhere, like an Escher drawing of gays where all the steps took people up and down simultaneously. A few silent men stood in the doorways of these small rooms, leaning against the architrave nonchalantly, looking calm and confident, their silence compounding their air of confidence – they would use just their eyebrows to occasionally gesture to someone as they walked past as if to say, 'All right?'

'All right' seemed like a much more appropriate energy to greet someone if one was attempting to act out the stereotype of masculinity. Much more in keeping than my inclination to say, 'Hellooo! How are you?!' or the more formal, 'How do you do?' or the more chatty, 'Watchya?' which my mum and dad's window cleaner said to me when he came into the kitchen to get his bucket filled (not a euphemism). Any of my more personality-laden greetings would have been way out of step with the masculine performances everyone was trying to honour. I feared that speaking at all in my much less masculine voice could upset their macho act and the whole performance would be revealed for what it was: no longer an illicit fantasy but just some plywood room dividers and a festoon of LEDs in the upstairs of a hot tub and snack shop.

The men in the doorways seemed to be staring off into the middle distance, like centurions in the Roman army. They ignored me, as I clearly wasn't fitting the role they had already cast in their minds. I wondered if I should hold myself in an even more upright way, pushing out my pigeon chest further, to try to seem more desirable. Though really I knew it was unlikely to help.

At the end of the corridor was a wall full of holes, at various heights and various sizes – presumably not the work of shoddy plastering, though. I cautiously peered through one of the holes to see what was happening on the other side. Nothing was happening. It was just an empty room – which, with hindsight, was lucky, as otherwise I could have lost an eye.

I heard grunting and slapping sounds coming from somewhere, so I guessed someone was having a good time. Either that or they were kneading bread dough. Through one of the open doors, I caught a glimpse of two men engaged in what looked to me more like the Heimlich manoeuvre. I didn't look for long as Mary Poppins taught me it is rude to stare, so I hurried on by.

Further on was an even more dimly lit room, which was empty, save for a large square of vinyl tarpaulin suspended from the ceiling with chains. If suspended higher up, it might have worked as some kind of uplighter or perhaps even a clever shelving system for use on a ship, but alas it was much lower down, which meant it was probably a sex swing.

It was unoccupied as was the rest of the room, giving me a chance to take in the interior choices: mirrors bedecked the walls, which my mother would have approved of as she maintains that mirrors always make a small space look larger whilst bringing light to dark corners. Wooden pillars supported the ceiling, which whilst offering a welcome alpine reference, felt out of place and whimsical in this otherwise industrial space. Frankly, the aesthetic didn't work: black vinyl, metal chains and brushed steel are surely based in 'postmodern factory', whereas the wood and mirrors resembled a ski lodge and a hairdresser's. The effect was a room that was confused – unsettling – gauche. It was little wonder that it remained unoccupied.

Over my shoulder and down the corridor, the Roman centurion kept guard on his part of the walkway, having still failed to make anyone's acquaintance.

Feeling despondent about the interiors, I felt a little tired, on account of it getting later in the evening, and a tad cold as I was wearing nothing but a towel. As I was too scared to engage in any of the activities that might keep me warm, I decided it was time to head back downstairs.

Walking swiftly back along the dim corridor with shoulders pinned back and chest puffed out, still trying to affect some sort of imagined masculine confidence, my foot failed to make purchase with the floor and so slipped out awkwardly in front of me. I could feel myself sliding out of control like a cartoon character in a chase scene, their assailant having poured oil on the road to turn them into a spinning mess and slow them down. Except for me, it was a sexual lubricant I had stepped in. As my right foot slid ahead of me, I was about to go over completely and reached for support from the plywood walls, and in moving so quickly, my towel almost fell away entirely. In a split second, I managed to reassert my balance, grab the towel just as it fell and regain my composure. The butch man in the doorway made eye contact just as I recovered my dignity, and I saw that he was giggling. I realised he wasn't so stern after all, and in making him laugh with me, I had completed my first slapstick comedy routine, and seen that there was more empathy here than I had realised.

I walked the rest of the corridor with caution at what lay under my feet but also with renewed confidence. I didn't want to go into the stern man's room, but I realised this wasn't such a frightening place after all.

Descending the stairs, I found myself back in the café area. It was like the whole complex had been designed to evoke a theme park with its different zones, as though there might be a Wild West area or a traditional Victorian high street around the next corner.

The café was busier now than before. Men of various ages sat on the bar stools and chesterfield sofas holding their cans of Coke and Club biscuits. I had a feeling of increased confidence from my lubed-up corridor experience, and the fact that I had managed to avoid doing myself an injury up there, but I knew I wanted to go home now.

I was frustrated that I had failed to do what you were supposed to do in a place like this. Yet again I had failed to keep up with what I imagined everyone else was doing and I pitied myself for being so pathetic. The times I went out on my own meant my harsh inner monologue could really take centre stage. Looking back on my younger self, though, I can have more compassion. I can feel a vague whisper of pride that I hadn't let fear stop me from finding out what was actually going on there. I had learnt that I didn't want to join in, but at least I could say I tried, and slowly, I was learning to accept that I didn't have to live up to the supposed expectations as laid out in those magazines.

I walked confidently back to the changing room, moving my hips freely and not trying to stick out my nipples. I quickly put my clothes back on, feeling like I had definitely had enough adventures for one day. I hurried out, not sure if I had ticked this adventure off or not.

On the train back home, Dad texted me: 'Are you OK? Let me know what time you're coming back and I can pick you up from the station.'

'I'm on the train now. See you at the station in 20?' I should have been standing on my own two feet, but in truth, I was delighted.

The steps we take as young adults can feel like strides away from where we started, turning our backs on those who raised us. These steps are, of course, necessary markers to prove to ourselves that we can follow our own instincts and stand on our own feet. Unless there's lube on the floor, of course.

'Everything all right?' he asked as I got into the passenger seat.

'Yeah, Dad.'

'The world takes you at your own valuation'

Life had taught Dad that if you walk into a room as though you're not worth anything, people will probably treat you as such. However, if you walk into a room with confidence, people will behave as though you're priceless!*

(*He might not have put it quite as theatrically as this.)

7

The best ass in New York City

I woke up on the floor of a Manhattan apartment surrounded by crockery. It was the home of my friend Lili, and I had come to America to make it, to finally be someone.

In my mid-twenties, I had been doing stand-up for about three years, and I still wasn't very good at all. My shows at the Edinburgh Fringe had been mediocre at best and I was still really sad most of the time because I couldn't work out how to get a boyfriend. I didn't know what I was supposed to be, and constant overthinking meant I ended up in a sort of paralysis, not able to see clearly what I was supposed to do next.

It pained me because I desperately wanted to be a success for my parents. My dad worked so hard, he always seemed so in control and he was so good at everything he turned his hand to, whether it was redecorating a room, tiling a floor, or even redoing the electrics of our house. He had the energy of a much younger man – he even had the energy to help me, who was desperately trying to have some sort of career. He would never say no to giving me a lift to the station, or picking up a parcel for me, all while making sure I had breakfast before I left and dinner when I came in.

I felt like I should know what I was doing. Other people my age seemed to; comics I had started out with were soaring in their work, but I couldn't even work out how to write a new routine. I decided I needed to go away to show that I could stand on my own two feet, away from my family, and prove that I could be a success.

So I went to America to make a change and make my fortune. It seemed like the sort of thing people did in movies, and it always worked out one way or another for them, so why shouldn't it work out for me? All in all, a host of insecurities and the inability to write new material turned out to be a terrible basis on which to spark a career in another country; I wasn't even sure of who I was at home. I didn't even have a plan of how I would launch myself, but I knew that if I could be the exuberant person I dreamed I could be, then somehow it would all work out.

New York seemed like the sort of place one would find some kind of self-assurance. It wasn't the most original plan, perhaps, given that it's the theme of most television sitcoms and films from the last part of the twentieth century. However, I knew from these fables that in America, nothing succeeds like confidence. It's infectious, the way people dream big, set out plans to achieve things and then go about achieving them all while eating hamburgers, talking fast and having a series of affairs. I knew it could rub off on me somehow, and sure enough, as soon as I arrived, I felt like I was finally the version of myself that I liked. No one knew me from back home and I was wearing my self-confidence like a new jumper (or sweater as I would have called it, trying to fit in in America) and I thought it really suited me.

This was a trip that was different to my previous time there. Unlike my first visit, when I was eighteen and had come to the city for a couple of days, this time I was determined not to be a wallflower who skulked around outside gay bars too scared to go in. This time I would be happy and exuberant!

Walking down the sidewalk of the hallowed Seventh Avenue – or 'fashion avenue', as it is sometimes dubbed – I saw a woman wearing the nicest overcoat I think I had ever seen. It was long and flowing and made of red panels of tapestry. 'Oh my!' I thought, affecting an American accent, even in my head. 'She looks amazing, and wow, she has got the expression of someone who I can tell has the sort of self-assurance I can relate to!' No longer would I be the sort of shy, awkward Brit who feared the world and made a fool of himself. Feeling almost flirtatious in my energy, I knew I had to tell this woman how great she looked – who doesn't love compliments?! So without a second thought, I yelled across the sidewalk, 'Oooh, I love your coat! What a great coat!'

I thought she would be delighted. New York always seemed like the sort of place you could just shout out nice things. The woman stared back at me with a stone-cold face of fury. It was as though, for some reason, she wasn't impressed by my delightfully eccentric camp English accent at all. She was behaving like the entire world did when I came out: she was staring, confused, as though what I had said was perfectly obvious and a waste of everyone's time.

It seemed like an unusual response, but I carried on strolling along the sidewalk. As I stopped at the crossing, a young woman stood alongside me and said, 'Do you know who you just yelled at?'

'No,' I said, shrugging innocently.

'That was Anna Wintour!' The young woman covered her mouth to stop herself screaming at the thought of my embarrassment and scuttled off ahead of me. My blood ran cold. I felt like I had just been stared at by the Ice Queen herself. I assuaged my horror by thinking, 'Well, maybe the editor-in-chief of all of Vogue's publications and the inspiration for *The Devil Wears Prada* might need the occasional compliment about her overcoat. I know I would!' I certainly did at this point. 'Oooooh I love your coat!' was basically what I'd shouted. She must've thought I was being sarcastic.

America is a complicated place, and New York just a small part of it. The main things I noticed about it was that everyone seemed to be dramatic and in the middle of some sort of crisis: whether it's their children underperforming at school, the threat of terrorism or what celebrities are up to that morning. Everyone was busy all the time, looking at their phones, rushing to a personal trainer or picking up their underperforming children.

American television shows reflect this and seem to be built around people having huge arguments. You know they are about to happen because the narrator mentions it at the start and then about seventeen times during the twenty-three minute show. The television shows also feature lots of crying and dramatic music, like the presenter is being followed around by their very own orchestra.

I am not surprised Americans are so stressed all the time: they don't have toilet cubicle doors. I was horrified when I first made this discovery. Instead, they have metal rectangles that don't align properly so there are sizeable gaps at the sides and they start much higher up and finish much lower at the top so you can see most, though not all, of the person in there. There isn't much privacy at all. People standing up after using the facilities pop out of the top like puppets. It is for this reason that I have never been able to go to the toilet during any of my visits to the United States.

Lili was a few years older than me and would not accept any money for letting me stay in her apartment. She and my friend Charlie had met on a bus tour of New Zealand a few years earlier and though I had only met her once, on her subsequent visit to London, she made me more welcome than I could ever have imagined in her home in Chelsea. Lili is kind and generous to a fault, which is no small feat in a city like New York. She is around my height, her heritage is Lebanese and she wears the best perfume, has the widest grin and laughs the best laugh. She is a magnet for interesting, quirky people and even people like me. I slept on the inflatable mattress in her living room and loved waking up to hear the roar of the traffic somewhere out there in the city and to see the tall buildings that surrounded the apartment.

If I was feeling uninspired at home, Lili was the perfect antidote because she threw me into the real side of New York. Not the version we see on films and TV shows. I loved all of it; the way it was noisy and a bit dirty, as well as glamorous and vibrant. It was a place where people lived – really lived. I wanted to be surrounded by this stuff forever. I wanted it to be my everyday, my humdrum. I wanted to be so immersed in all of it that I was bored with it all.

While I was also staying there, Lili had lent her one-bedroom apartment out to an amateur group of ceramicists she'd met when she was working as a backpack salesperson in Las Vegas. Quickly renamed by me as the Crockery Sisters, these three women in their fifties with flowing kaftans, greying up-dos and uptight attitudes were fascinating to me.

They looked like hippy creative types, but they seemed extremely highly strung. 'We'll need the apartment for four days, and you can't touch anything – there'll be pieces everywhere.' 'Pieces' were what they called what looked to me like rough grey lumps of glazed sludge. One of the sludges had a wire sticking out of it and a lampshade balanced on top and was being sold as a lamp for the same cost as my flight across the Atlantic. Their thin smiles barely concealed their constant sense of anguish as they informed us that 'it would make a huge difference to us if you could be out of the apartment as much as possible while we're setting up . . . ?'

That afternoon, we went out for hours to keep out of their way, and Lili took me on a whistle-stop tour of the city like Mary Poppins does with the Banks children. We first went to see her friend, the artist Barton Lidice Beneš. Lili told me before we met him that 'he's the oldest man in New York with AIDS', and whether or not this was true, he was a man who had lived through the first generation of the epidemic, lost his lover to the disease and had himself lived with AIDS since the mid-eighties. Rather than shy away from it, he embraced it in his work, even using drops of his blood to make work that confronted people with the crisis, their fears and their mortality.

He lived in the most extraordinary building. It was a rent-controlled commune of artists in a block of apartments over-looking the Hudson River. When we arrived, he was making beautiful work with paper butterflies. The space was crammed full of artworks and equipment he was using to cut up the paper. Rather than a bed, he slept on Persian carpets stacked up on a dais on one side of the room. He was frail and moved slowly, but he laughed heartily and with a slight wheeze perhaps, because he had smoked from an early age, even when he was on the US Olympic speed skating team. That was the sort of existence he had lived, packed full of life, always interested in people – even me, who had little more than a dream and a few weeks to spend in New York. He took the trouble to chat with me about what I was up to. He was supportive and didn't once shame me for not knowing what the hell I was doing.

Next on our list of activities was a small party organised by two gay guys who lived in an expensive apartment on the Upper

West Side: Roger and Walter. They were doing 'something with lobster', apparently. Walter was approximately twenty years older than Roger; Walter made a lot of money working for a bank, Roger made a lot of time to spend it. Most recently, he had been spending it on sending himself on a wine course, and as a result, was very keen to let everyone know about it.

They were the sort of couple who were always on the go, busy doing things, flying to places, organising parties, having meetings, walking dogs, tasting wine, and consequently spoke directly and, to my sensitive little soul, seemed like they were angry. Maybe they were having a disagreement amongst themselves and the shock waves of their argument could still be felt as you got near. Who knew? There was no time to ask!

'Darling, wonderful to see you,' Walter said, embracing Lili.

'Hellooo!' said Lili warmly. 'This is Tom.'

'Hi-come-in'. The words rushed together, no hand shaking – no time! These were proper New Yorkers and their abruptness was part of their charm.

'Shoes!' he said with alarm.

'We'll take our shoes off, don't worry – it's a shoes-off kind of place!' said Lili, smiling.

Shuffling into the sitting room, we met a small gathering of people. Apart from our hosts, there was Walter's mother Barbara, dressed in a tennis skirt, who stood inspecting the buffet table while her friend Cynthia sat in an armchair, not speaking but looking at the floor with the air of someone constantly concerned. The neighbours Paul and Gerald sat on a sofa that was slightly too low down so their knees on their long legs seemed to be higher than their heads. Both were in their fifties with dark hair styled in the way that all New York men seem to have it: brushed forward and spiked slightly, yet perfectly, at the front. Perfect hair was combined with perfect bright white teeth and polo shirts with the collars popped. I got the sense that they would be a laugh if you met them on a night out, but tonight there would be no messing around: it was best behaviour for their uptight neighbours, so they sat quietly on the couch.

Despite only eight of us being present, the small front room felt overcrowded, especially as half of it was taken up by a table covered in lobsters on the half-shell. The table's leaves had been opened up to make it even larger to accommodate not just lobster but also prawns, huge mounds of salads and grilled vegetables and a board of cheeses placed on vine leaves, alongside small, crisp rice crackers.

We said our hellos efficiently, and then the room slumped into silence and I immediately panicked that we wouldn't have anything to talk about. What if the whole night was just all of us sat here in silence, staring at the table piled high with so much crustacea it was like an exhibit at the Natural History Museum about prehistoric creatures? Luckily, Lili is very good at starting conversations. On sitting down, she looked at Walter's mother, Barbara, and exclaimed, 'Walter!' Everyone turned. 'Your mother has *the* best ass in New York City. I swear to God!' The woman must have been eighty years old.

New Yorkers are earnest at the best of times, and so surprisingly didn't laugh at this unusual compliment but instead turned to look at said ass themselves and then nodded in agreement, muttering, 'It's true.'

'So true,' said Gerald, shaking his head in agreement.

'Such a great ass . . .' echoed Paul.

'Thank you, dear,' said Barbara coyly.

'Spin around! Show it to us!' instructed Lili boldly. Barbara was only too happy to oblige and began her delicate twirl, with her arms in the air like the china ballet dancer on a wind-up music box.

'Barbara, how do you keep it so tight?' Lili implored. The assembled gathering looked to her intently; they needed to know!

The old woman, now holding onto the back of an armchair, said, 'Well, I play tennis most days, so that helps, I guess?'

'Look at it! I could leave my drink on top of it.' Lili was sitting next to me as she said it, so the ass in question was at my eye height, but, being British, I thought it might be impertinent to place my drink on it, and if anything I didn't know where to look so I gazed over the buffet and out of the window.

'Would anyone like a glass of wine?!' said Roger like a gazelle with a tray, as he leapt out of the kitchen parading a collection of wine glasses and three bottles of 'gorgeous wine from the Napa Valley!'

Roger knelt down in front of the coffee table and placed his tray and glasses down. He did it without really having to steady himself, which suggested to me he had a lot of time to work on his core strength at yoga classes. He placed a pouring spout in the top of the bottle and began to portentously serve the wine, swirling each glass as he went along. 'It really needs to aerate – I should have opened it sooner.' He was clearly proud to share with us all his new-found knowledge, whereas really I just wanted to get drunk.

In marked contrast to British parties, where you are encouraged to drink as much as you can as quickly as possible in order to relax, it seemed that our hosts were not so bothered about anyone relaxing. We were going to have to sit here with just one small glass of wine each, sipping dribbles of it to appreciate its tannins. 'Let's start with the Pinot Noir,' he said archly, sticking his nose into his glass. I was immediately depressed.

Walter sipped his Pinot and then got stuck into the conversation, direct as ever. 'Lil, I've got to tell you – our beach house? Renovation?! Terrible time! Worst experience of our lives, right, Roger?'

'Sure was, these contractors, I mean—' said Roger, swilling his glass by the base now and holding it up to the light, gesturing to everyone else to do the same.

'Oh, don't get me started on the contractors,' moaned Walter, 'I don't want to ruin the night, but let's just say they have been *the worst*. The whole thing – *total* nightmare!'

'Oh, I bet it has – contractors are just the worst,' said Lili. The idea of having a beach house, never mind the finances to renovate it, seemed wonderful though, so I couldn't quite understand why a person would be so upset about it. I could only assume they were being filmed for a forthcoming television show called something like *Wealthy People's Contractors from Hell!*

'Tom . . . you're a comedian?' Walter demanded across the group, snapping me out of my daydream about owning a beach house.

'Yes.' The room looked at me in silence. 'Well, trying to be . . . haha!'

Everyone stared. Barbara looked disappointed that the conversation had moved on so quickly from her glorious posterior. Cynthia looked concerned again, and knocked back her glass of wine in one go. Gazing forlornly at the carpet, Barbara rubbed her tush briefly, like Aladdin did with his lamp, before slumping into a chair and tucking into a cracker.

'The comedy game? How's it going?' asked Walter expectantly. At home, I would feel much more comfortable looking remorseful and explaining that it wasn't going very well at all and could barely make a living. In fact, I sometimes stayed in bed until three o'clock in the afternoon. However, in America, in this apartment, things were different. At this point in my life, I didn't have the experience to know I could just speak loudly to evoke confidence, nor that I could make fun of a person in a way that would make them laugh.

Instead, I tried to just pretend I was successful, albeit with a quieter voice. 'Yeah, I – erm – it's going OK, thanks. I've done some stuff on radio and I'm gigging in places around Britain.'

Everyone looked embarrassed and I wished we could go back to discussing the benefits of tennis for your ass. 'You're on BBC TV? That sort of thing?'

'Well, actually I did win a competition with the BBC . . . it was on the radio, though.'

'Right . . . right.'

'This lobster is amazing! Thank you very much for inviting me to your beautiful home – it's really all so stunning.' I expected everyone to join me in agreement and we could talk about something else, but everyone just looked embarrassed that I had broken the secret rule and complimented the hosts. It was the worst thing I could have done because this clearly showed that I wasn't used to fancy lobster parties, and therefore wasn't remotely successful like them.

'Tom has a blog and a website, and he's doing some great stuff on Twitter,' Lili broadcast to the room, full of positivity, beaming with pride. The room looked even more disappointed; they thought they would be getting John Cleese, not some under-confident British schmuck with nothing going for him, and to top it all, he'd come and tried to avail himself of their lobster! Extra lobster that Tushie-Grandma Barbara could have had as a salad the next day after tennis!

That night at Lili's, I slept amongst the crockery. It was sinister to think it was out there in the darkness, watching me as I tried to nod off. The dishes and sculptures all made slight movements throughout the night, causing strange noises like it was talking to me, with its croaky voice. 'You're a failure! Go home!' it hoarsely whispered. I worried it might fall and shatter on the floor, a rogue shard bouncing into my inflatable mattress, causing it to explode and for me to be jettisoned across the room and impaled on that lamp.

Lili told me that she would be going away with work for a few days and so I would have the apartment to myself. On my first morning alone I pretended for a moment that I was living there like any other New Yorker. I made myself a coffee and held it with both hands like people do in coffee commercials. I had decided that my futile attempts to message industry people about meeting me were a waste of time. Where would I even start?

I was enjoying my time there anyway, meeting so many people and pretending I lived there full time, pretending I was a confident person, sauntering about in New York with no job. I looked out of the window and thought about having pancakes for breakfast. Perhaps I would read the *New Yorker* or book tickets for something at the Guggenheim. I felt so American. Then the electric buzzing sound of the doorbell cut through my fantasy.

'Hello?' I said tentatively over the intercom to the front door.

'Tom?' said the voice. 'It's Nelly. Lil's friend? Did she tell you I'd be coming by?'

'Err, no, I don't think—'

'Can I come up?'

'Oh sure, yeah,' and I buzzed the button with the key on it, panicking about who this person would be.

Opening the front door to the apartment, I saw Nelly clattering along the corridor with several large suitcases and bags.

'Nelly, it's so nice to meet you – I'm Tom,' I said, holding the door open for her to bring all her things in.

'Oh, hi, buddy!' she said sweetly and energetically. 'Can you help me with my stuff?' she asked as she left half of it in the hallway.

'Yes, of course!' I said obligingly, trying to be like Hugh Grant, while secretly thinking, 'What is going on here?' and 'What heavy bags!' We both dragged the suitcases and rucksacks into the apartment. Nelly immediately made me nervous because she was so gung-ho about manoeuvring past the crockery while I followed, slowly, trying desperately not to nudge a sculpture onto the floor, ready to dive forward to catch anything that Nelly might knock. It was like she didn't even see these fragile creatures, which, by this point, had become croaky little people, lulling me to sleep each night with their critical thoughts.

'Lili tells me you work as a comedian?'

'Yes, that's right,' I said, hauling the last of the bags into the apartment and heaving them onto the living room floor.

'Oh, I don't understand comedy at all – just don't get it. Maybe I haven't got the attention span or something?'

'Oh yeah, well, maybe.'

'Did Lil tell you about my new invention? It's a vibrating mat for healing and for spiritual realignment. I need some help taking it to the convention centre for a show there? Lil said you wouldn't mind helping?'

'Oh sure – yes, of course, I remember now!' I said, lying, and concerned that in pretending so hard to be a natural New Yorker I had not listened to Lili telling me this.

'I'll show you how it works if you like?'

'Err, OK – yes, please!' I feigned enthusiasm.

'It's fine' she said, unfurling the mechanical mat on the floor, 'we can still talk.'

'Oh sure, OK!' I said, even though at this point I was ready for the conversation to end. Before I knew it, Nelly had plugged it in, slipped off her sandals and lay on it before I could get away.

'It just takes a moment to warm up – could you make me a tea? Like an 'erbal tea?'

'Yeah, sure,' I shouted, to be heard over the now-whirring machine, which was sounding like a hoover, with tubes sucking air into it and pushing it out again as the vibrating began.

'Oh God!' Nelly screamed, almost orgasmically. 'It's happening.' On the word 'happening', she transmogrified into a robot. Not literally, but she sounded like one, the machine making her voice metallic, much deeper and much more echoey; it quivered menacingly as the electronic shivering began.

I returned with her tea to find Robot-Nelly lying on the floor in the sitting room, vibrating away on the floorboards. I very much worried that her mechanical shaking might send her incrementally along until she flew straight into the pottery display delicately placed on one of the side tables. She wasn't worried. She very much wanted to talk. 'I gueeeeesszzsss Lllilll tolllld-dddd you abouttt whattt's happppennnedd?'

How had I missed so many details? 'Well, no, not rea—'

'My huuuussssband and I have been going through some troubled timezzzz,' she went on with her vibro-speech. 'The marrrriaaaaage is faaaaaalling apaaaaart reeeeally – I found other mennnnn's undddddddderweaaaaaar in his suitcassssssse.'

'My, well, that is a lot to process . . .' I said, referring to her situation and also myself. 'How much would that shelf of pottery cost if it fell on the floor and smashed?' I wondered as Nelly trembled ever closer to the pottery. It would be thousands and, since they were American, they might sue me for the money – I'd be bankrupt!

Nelly was still talking, 'Iiiit allllllll starrrrrrrrrted wheeeennnnnn thaaaaaaaaat bird flllewwww throooooooooough ourrrr bed-rooooooom windoooooooowwww: it smaaaaaaaashed the mirrrroooooooor!'

'Right?' I said, nodding empathetically.

'I haaaaaaaaaave theeeeeeese dreeeeeeeams wherrrrrrrrre IIIIIII'm gettttttttttting furrrrrrrtherrrrrr aaaaaaaaaand furrr-rrrrrrtherrrrrr awaaaaaaaaay frommmmmmm himmmmmm. Dooooooo yooooou thinnnnnnk thaaaaaat meeeeeeans some-thingggggggggg?'

'Well, possibly, I'm not a psychic or anything, but maybe.'

'Yoooooou're riiightt – probably nothing,' she trembled.

And with that the mat stopped shaking, the alignment com-plete, and Nelly sprung back to standing.

'Can you help me? I have to get to my conference, and I just can't work out where it is and I need help with all the equipment and the mat. Do you know where the conference centre is near here?'

'I mean, I don't live here, so no—'

' . . . It's just that Lil said you'd be able to help . . .' She stared at me.

'Give me a second, and I'll put my shoes on and maybe I can help you find it. Do you know where it is?'

'No, that's why I asked!' she replied cheerily.

'No, but is there an address, I meant?'

'Oh, yes. It says here' – she held out a scrap of paper with biro scribbled on it – 'that it's Tenth Avenue and Forty-Eighth Street, but I just can't work the map.'

I've never worked a map; in fact, I've mainly just read maps. 'OK. I can walk you there,' I said, shuffling my heel into a shoe.

Walking along the nine blocks to the conference centre took about thirty minutes. 'Gee, for a visitor, you really know your way round this city.'

It's a grid system; all you have to do is be able to count. 'I guess I sure do!' I exclaimed. We walked for most of it in silence, and then three minutes later, 'Here we are then!'

'*Great!*' beamed Nelly and she held her arms out to hug me. 'It's been so great to meet you!' she said as she held me in an embrace for slightly too long and then clattered her way into the conference centre to sell her vibrating mats.

Lili took me to meet her father, Hank. We bought lox and bagels and took them to his apartment. Hank was a tall man who looked like Sean Connery and who had a habit of leaving his apartment door open. We walked straight in. Born in the mid-1930s, he had a lot of life experience and a lot of love to give – 'Arab hospitality – you'll see!' said Lili.

'Come in, come in!' He welcomed us both and immediately hugged me. 'Ah, whatcha brought me? Bagels?? My favourite!' He beamed down, looking at the food with a chuckle.

'We got the pumpernickel ones from Murray's. You like those?'

'Sure, I do – come on, let's eat!'

'Hank' – Lili called her dad by his name – 'you know I saw Barbara the other night – the one with the firm tush?'

'Oh yeah, sure, I remember her – she OK?'

'Same as ever – ass like a sideboard!'

'Oh, and a son to match too, huh?'

Hank was the opposite of the uptight Upper West Side gays from the other night. I loved Hank immediately, like I had known him my whole life.

'I've got to get a haircut,' said Hank, which was an unusual thing for a bald man in his late seventies to say.

'You should take Tom with you,' said Lili, now suggesting that two bald men go to the barber's.

'We should go to the barber's!' he exclaimed. 'Come on, when you've finished your bagel, let's take bikes and we'll cycle over the bridge. Take Lil's bike – she won't mind – it's here, anyhow.'

'I'd be delighted!' I said, trying to stuff as much of the bagel into my mouth as possible while trying not to think about how horrified my mother would be. She hated the idea of me walking anywhere, never mind cycling – too dangerous!

Hank and I cycled over the Brooklyn Bridge for our unnecessary haircuts. Although it wasn't totally pointless, as we did end up going so fast on the Brooklyn Bridge cycle path that we almost took off. Hank walked me into his barber's in Brooklyn, tucked away at the start of Brooklyn Heights. It was a small shop overcrowded with photos of haircuts that no one had asked for in twenty years. His tall frame towered in the small space as he greeted the men who must have been thirty-five years his junior, but who welcomed him like he had grown up with them. They trimmed his close crop of hair and tidied up my short beard while we chatted about nothing and sat comfortably in silence. It was a far cry from the bright lights of the bustling city just across the bridge. Afterwards, Hank took me to Sahadi's, the Middle Eastern grocery store tucked away down on Cobble Hill to pick up dried fruits and spices like dukka. 'You know, my mother used to come here,' he told me as we pottered among the jars of pistachios and whole counters holding different types of olives. 'The spices are OK, but it's not as good as the stuff you get in Lebanon. You can't get food like that here. Problem is, they don't like you bringing bags of strange powders into the country!'

Having finished our shopping, we fastened our helmets under our chins and turned our bikes around to head back. 'You ready?' he said as he powered off fearlessly from the sidewalk and began pedalling. We sped across the bridge and down into the city. I lost Hank somewhere in China Town, as he let the momentum of the downhill path coming off the bridge sweep him along and back up through the city, our freshly shaved and polished heads making us all the more aerodynamic. Hank moved without touching the pedals as he glided along the streets like a superhero, his mac billowing behind him in the breeze. I managed to override my mother's voice telling me that one false move or a car door opening and I'd be somersaulted through the air and spend the rest of my life paralysed and living in an iron lung or something. I was desperate to keep up and pedalled and pedalled but couldn't quite catch up with him. Every time, he seemed to be turning a corner just ahead of me. It didn't matter; I knew I'd meet up with him, eventually. It felt great to be going so fast without a care in the world. All the petty worries about what I was supposed to be doing with my little life didn't matter. Going fast on a bike and keeping up with Hank was all that mattered.

I finally caught up with Hank back at his apartment. He was completely relaxed and not out of breath in the slightest. I knew I had made a friend, and I knew that out of me and the man knocking on eighty, I was the old man. However, I was exhilarated. I realised that much as I liked the characters and fast-paced world of Manhattan, I think I felt more at home with Hank pottering around the ordinary world of barbers and supermarkets. He reminded me of home; a man born before the Second World

War, who had seen life, worked hard and raised a family – he was a version of my dad. I hadn't truly felt like I was part of this city until I had found the equivalent of my home life, confirming that whether by car or by bike, all roads really do lead to home.

My few weeks in New York came to an end on Halloween. I had never seen anywhere as excited as New York was about 31st of October. Windows held skeletons and witches, whilst every doorstep seemed to be furnished with a selection of pumpkins, and some even had their whole front door garlanded with autumnal plants and flowers. People in New York seemed stressed as they hung out their decorations, but as I knew now, they weren't happy unless they were stressed.

The costume parade was taking place that night, starting in Greenwich Village, and I decided that I had to be a part of this event somehow. There was a spirit in the air. It was going to be electric and it was going to be memorable and more than that, it was definitely going to be fun.

I often saw big, burly men walking around Chelsea, looking terrifying, until I glanced down to see their small dogs immaculately groomed at their feet. 'Hello, darling, how are you?!' they said to one another, kissing on both cheeks (and some of them were bending over at the time). On the morning of Halloween, I noticed they weren't out and about as they usually were. On my stroll to get a coffee and generally mooch around, I found a lot of the familiar faces were heading to a small park with their pooches. Entering the park, I saw a big crowd assembled by the dog pen. I was gobsmacked at what I had stumbled upon. A small tent had been erected with a sign above it: *Doggy Halloween Parade*. Underneath, judges sat at a table in front of which a grand promenade was taking place: pompous and ceremonious in equal measure. A pug dressed as Queen Elizabeth I graced the head of the parade, a greyhound as a Pierrot clown danced its way along behind, followed by a Yorkshire terrier as a pirate, a bulldog with legs attached to become a spider, even a Labrador dressed as Anne Boleyn.

I was amazed. If this was how seriously the dogs took it, I could only imagine what to expect from the human parade that night. I would have to really up my game if I was going to walk in it and not be upstaged by a springer spaniel I'd seen that morning. The trouble was, I was too late; people had been planning their outfits for months. The Halloween stores that had sprung up around the city had huge queues around the block and at this stage only really held the dregs of their selection, essentially plastic packs with costumes consisting of normal jobs prefixed with 'sexy'. 'Sexy secretary' being the most obvious one. The others included 'sexy dentist', 'sexy German' and, bizarrely perhaps, 'Sexy supermarket worker' – essentially a tabard and some fishnet stockings.

Already people were running around the city in their outfits. They were so witty! So intelligently thought out! People danced across the street dressed as tables and aspidistras – there was an entire medieval court sauntering out of a side street. Barriers were being put up along the route – it was going to be a huge event!

I knew I had to dash to the Halloween store to see what they had left. I couldn't let myself down. This was my big trip to prove to myself and the world that I was a confident person. Maybe I would make new friends, meet a new boyfriend, perhaps? We could have a relationship over long distance (which would be perfect, as that way I wouldn't have to introduce him to my mum and dad). Maybe I'd meet someone who could help me with my career – there must be someone around who could offer me some kind of leg-up. The store didn't have much left at all, except for a few wigs and a selection of various glasses.

Walking out of the bathroom later that evening, I stood proudly in the middle of the room, surrounded by crockery. I tried to seem like the most confident version of myself that I could muster, wearing Lili's big coat, the bobbed nylon wig and cheap oversized sunglasses I had bought from the costume store. I was Anna Wintour, and no one was stealing my confidence today.

*'Look what I just dug up, Tom — these potatoes! . . .
They're a gift from God!'*

Dad was always amazed at what the garden might produce.
He hadn't planted the potatoes that year and yet they had self-
sown so he brought them in excitedly to show me. He couldn't
believe it.

8

Times are hard

I used to think I was born as an older soul, and so during my teenage years felt I was probably in my mid-forties. Now, as I approach my forties, I feel more like I am at retirement age, contemplating how best to fill my time. What would I do with myself if I wasn't working? Even now, the idea of filling a day in a productive way seems so exhausting. Never mind a whole week. I suppose spending it with other people would make a day seem worthwhile. Helping others? Isn't that what we're supposed to find fulfilling? Just being out and about might be enough. Time in the garden, I think, would make me believe I was achieving something. I have often found it helpful to keep a diary, sometimes to get my emotions on the page, but at other times, just to prove that I have definitely done something at all.

Monday
My Aunt Pearl, my mum's sister, has come over from Australia. It is the first time she could get here since pandemic restrictions were lifted. I took them both to the Chelsea Flower Show. They have been known to talk so much when they see each other they lose their voices. There was a long queue to collect tickets. We were sandwiched between Sarah Greene from *Blue Peter* and Gaby Roslin. Everyone was in good spirits, and I always find anything

garden related very calming – after all, you cannot plant geraniums or pick roses angrily. An elegant lady at the front carried an
umbrella covered in nylon roses, which flared out at the top in a
frilly way like she had just stepped out of the painting in *Mary
Poppins* or the racing scene in *My Fair Lady*. She wasn't so happy
about the queue, though.

I took Mum and Pearl for a coffee and a croissant. Mum said,
'No jam?' I told her not to start. She was joking, but I already
felt heart palpitations as a result of trying to make sure they both
had a perfect day, which was not necessary because they were
already quite happy having a coffee with the prospect of mooch-
ing around some nice gardens. I felt like I had to offer them more
somehow. Being an adult has often seemed like it's about making
sure everyone else is happy. It's a never-ending job.

The day went smoothly. A huge metal RAF pilot sculpture
from the Second World War looked up to the sky. We walked
through a display of roses that smelled so sweet. We went to see
Dan and Tayshan, who I met last year at my first time here at
the show. They had created a space called 'Hands Off Mangrove'
inspired by the real-life stories of the Mangrove Nine. The circle
of stone seats at the centre offered a space that seemed healing; it
felt peaceful to be there. I chatted to Joanna Scanlan by the Life-
boat Institute garden and we talked about the virtues of living
in suburbia and how I should persevere with Tom Wolfe's *The
Electric Kool-Aid Acid Test*. I bought a lamp to go in my garden at
home, which I didn't want really, but since Mum and Pearl had
talked to the man at the stand for so long, I thought I should buy
something. As my credit card was in the machine and the payment was going through, I casually said, 'Do you have a bag?' To
which he casually said, 'No.' So I had to carry it round the whole
show like I was Florence Nightingale.

We saw people starting to assemble around the south gate, so I couldn't help but do the same in case we missed something. I think everyone hoped it would be a member of the royal family. Cars arrived and people got out wearing big hats and accompanied by posh men (I have realised that I can spot posh men quite easily because they often have what look like quite scruffy suits on with baggy pockets and baggy shoulders). I think we saw lots of the Queen's cousins and some people I had never seen before in my life who I can only assume were ambassadors. I wondered if they sensed the disappointment in the crowd as they arrived. Must be a terrible way to get out of a car: 'We were hoping for the Queen!' people seemed to be saying. The disappointment made even more palpable because the chances of seeing her out and about are so rare these days.

We bumped into Carol Klein at the junction of the main avenue where the big show gardens meet the grandeur of the Royal Hospital. Carol is my favourite gardening presenter because she really believes in what she's saying. She's also so full of life, and last year when we were there, she got my parents and I pissed in a tent selling rosé. Probably one of the happiest days ever. Especially as Dad had said he didn't want to come, but we begged him to join, and when he was there, he loved it. Carol and Dad got along like a house on fire, and we got so drunk and stayed much later than we should have done and even tried to help ourselves to a glass of champagne from the bankers' reception happening in the main tent, but we got told to step away.

Seeing her this year, the first thing she said was, 'Where's Dad?!'

I explained we lost him at the end of last year. She looked heartbroken. We talked for a while. Mum went in for a hug and broke down fully, embracing her for a while. Strangely, I felt suddenly very old-fashioned and wanted to say, 'Oh, don't make a scene, Mother!' but Carol always seems like someone who's at home with emotions.

Suddenly, in the midst of tearful embraces, people in the corner were lifting their phones in the air as though filming something. I always think people look like they are doing a Roman salute when they do this. The commotion from the crowd grew louder, and then through the small throng of people, to polite applause, the late Queen arrived in a golf buggy. It was like a dream, really. She was sitting on the opposite side of the buggy, so we couldn't quite see her, but then as the buggy drove across the top of the avenue, she leant forward and the sun shone on her grey hair, and suddenly it was unmistakable that she was there. I didn't take a photo. Auntie Pearl said afterwards, 'Why would you want a photograph? She's on every stamp!'

We tried to hail a taxi to get home, but it was so busy. 'I'm so sorry – I think I've messed this up for you. I didn't plan how we would get home, did I?' Mum and Pearl didn't seem to mind at all. I think I put myself under pressure to make everything perfect but no one minded, really. It was just nice to be out all together. Got home exhausted with a lamp in hand.

Despite tiredness, I still checked for slugs in the garden. My vegetable patch didn't look nearly as neat or as productive as the ones at the Flower Show. The slug situation was worse than I expected, as though the slugs and snails were having their own Glastonbury on the leaves of my garden peas. It was raining and I had nothing but the light on my phone. I didn't want to touch them, as they looked so horrible and I imagined felt even worse, so I tried to use my small shovel to get them off. I saw the beer traps – small bowls of beer to entice the slugs – had been working and were now a disgusting slurping swamp of dead slugs.

It took ages to manoeuvre them off each leaf, and I kept swearing in the wet darkness as I then had to dig among the leaves of the Swiss chard and carrots to locate where they had fallen. In digging deep in the undergrowth, I kept brushing past the other ones still clinging on. It was taking too long, so I ended up forcing myself to get over my fear of what they felt like and just grabbed them and threw them in the bush. Each one still made me scream, as I could sense them moving as I gripped them lightly between my thumb and finger. So many of them – the more I looked, the more there were, some of whom were shimmying up the actual bean poles, which didn't have anything growing up them – like overexcited rock stars about to stage-dive on a crowd of garden vegetables.

I poured a line of salt around the edge of the raised vegetable bed to try to put them off and then realised I had probably created some sort of satanic pentagram around the vegetables. I also looked in my book about allotments and saw that the salt can brush into the earth and contaminate it, killing the plants you're trying to protect. So I then went out with a dust pan and brush trying to collect the salt back in. I felt ridiculous.

As I got in the door, I saw my gardening gloves on the side and realised I could have used them to avoid the horrible feeling of touching the slugs. Went to bed exhausted from policing my tiny kingdom.

Tuesday
I woke up tired but had to be ready for a nurse who was coming round to perform a medical for the life insurance I wanted to sign up to. She was chatty and told me I should actually put out chillies, egg shells and coffee to deter the slugs. She took my blood pressure and said it was a little high, probably owing to the

slugs and starting the week navigating the world's most famous flower show with my mother and aunt alongside the UK's longest-reigning monarch.

I had to give a urine sample, which took me ages, as I had just gone and then had the pressure of knowing she was waiting in the other room for me to produce it. I can never go when I am under pressure; it was like those bathrooms in America all over again. Not only was the nurse waiting, but I also had the piano tuner coming at eleven, so I knew I couldn't be late. I once accidentally made Dad and my brother miss the train from one of my brother's football tournaments because I knew they were waiting for me outside the toilet and I just couldn't go. Determined not to repeat this, I eventually managed to relieve myself. The nurse then did the urine test using the test tube and some sort of litmus paper, balancing them on the parquet floor of the sitting room. It came back all fine, but to be honest, I was more concerned about spilling it on the floor. Especially with the piano tuner due any minute. What on earth would he think of me? She then bagged up all the detritus, including the urine sample, and told me to just put it all in my normal bin. It was a bit depressing to put a vial of my own piss in my kitchen bin. I was just staring at the bin, having completed the task, when I saw the piano tuner outside, raincoat hugged around him, backpack over one shoulder.

The weather has been sunny and then stormy, flitting from early summer sunshine to torrential downpour. I like this time of the year, as it's lush and newly green. It feels equatorial, tropical even, to have humidity and leaves along with gloomy skies and rain. It's good for making my way through scented candles.

The piano tuner was on good form, and I wanted to talk to him for ages about the best piano manufacturers before I realised that this was probably irritating and I was just being needy and he probably wanted to get on with tuning the piano.

Seeing that I still had my schoolboy grade pieces out on the music stand, he asked, 'Oh, are you doing grades?'

'Oh no, I've done them!' This was literally the only time that passing piano exams has ever had any bearing on my adult life.

'So you just left them out to impress me then?' I suppose in a way he was right; subconsciously, I probably had.

Had to leave him to it as I had to record my *Like Minded Friends* podcast with Suzi. Suzi calmed me down.

Wednesday

It has felt like I am cramming every moment with things this week. It dawned on me that for these first few months since losing Dad, I've been in shock and never really dealt with my feelings at all. I thought it was all going well, but now it feels like it's surfaced. Not as an explicit sadness but I think I still expect him to come back. There's a part of me that still turns to see him coming in the door. There's an instinct every now and then that I want to text him or ask his advice on the leak in the washing machine or what to do about the broken bathroom light switch upstairs.

The loss is too much to understand. A totemic figure in your life can't just disappear in the blink of an eye. If I told you to look out of the window now and you saw a building and then turned back to reading this and then I told you, 'That building isn't there any more,' and you looked back and the building had vanished without trace, it would seem like physics was broken or that our empirical understanding of the world couldn't be trusted. Something can't be there, here with us, and then suddenly not be here at all. That doesn't make any sense.

I think my inability to process it has been manifesting as anxiety — worries that are more amplified than usual. Outlandish fears about health and an extreme tiredness make me feel like I haven't got the energy to be upbeat in work meetings and day-to-day interactions. I just want to sleep all the time.

I find myself worrying about everything and tend to catastrophise, especially the things that I can't control: how are we going to stop inflation? If it keeps going up, will any of us be able to afford anything? Will it lead to disaster like the hyperinflation in Germany that helped lead to the rise of the Nazis? Concerning as this is, there is very little I can do about it and I would be better off thinking about the slugs really.

I panic about people on social media who seem similar to me, like they'll take over my identity, whatever that is — not just in work but take my place in the world somehow. I feel like I'm not enough. And if I give any of it up, I shall be giving over my place; someone else will do the work and I shall be replaced. Then what will I do? You can't exist if you don't have an identity.

I worry about how, in work, you have to be not just better but also louder. You have to be loudest! But maybe I'm losing my voice! I know this is nonsense and just my brain playing tricks on me because I am tired. Everyone is different and unique; there is space for everyone to work; it's exciting to see new people doing new things. I know this. I think I'm just scared of everything at the moment and I don't quite have the energy to fake confidence.

I'd go on antidepressants, but everyone keeps saying I'll regret it because they'll stop me from feeling and I need to feel all of these things to process the loss. Maybe I am being dramatic, as usual. Dad wouldn't want me to be dramatic.

Saw a text message from Dad about how a parcel arrived and it was my piano stool. Saw him there. Saw a shadow move behind me as I removed the slugs. Heard someone or something moving in the shrubs. Probably an animal. Probably the water dripping off the tree above. Wanted to text him back.

Left for the airport as performing in Jersey tonight.

Thursday

Jersey Airport sells potatoes. It is part of the duty-free since this is the product they are most famous for: Jersey Royal Potatoes. 'The Best in the World!'

'It doesn't make any sense,' I moaned to Alf. 'They sell them at the supermarket at home; why would you want to lug them back from here?'

I bought some anyway. I was flying back from a gig and Alf had come with me. I pinch myself whenever I get to travel for my job. It was always my dream to go to different places and see the world and meet different people. The pandemic made me appreciate what a privilege it is to travel and to roam freely. I am very lucky to be travelling, looking out on the sea and the sky and doing a job I love.

Jersey is beautiful. However, the waiting area at the airport gate is probably the worst place I have ever been in my whole entire life. And I have been to Wetherspoons in Bromley South.

We were told to make our way to the gate, as our flight was boarding. However, on arriving at the gate, we soon realised that the flight wasn't boarding at all, but rather we were just being held in some kind of overcrowded chamber. It was the most depressing space I had ever seen. Aside from not having enough chairs, most of which looked tired and uncomfortable anyway, the room managed to conjure up the spirit of a forgotten-about cupboard. I was incandescent with rage – the world can be so much nicer than this! People deserve so much better! Dark stains scarred the thin carpet and the windows were amber with grime, as though someone had lived here for an eternity, smoking sixty cigarettes a day. Aside from the yellowing of the windows, thick dust collected in the corners and the stainless-steel surrounding the windows failed to live up to its name and instead stood looking depressingly stained. Damp-looking patches besmirched the polyester ceiling tiles, which looked like they hadn't been replaced for decades.

Similar dark patches had infected the corners and spread their dull stains across the walls, even spreading to the middle to meet a patch where a can of drink had presumably exploded with misplaced excitement and splashed up it. No one had cleaned it, or even seemed to notice. Perhaps it was blood, spilled from someone finding the room so depressing that they had self-immolated using whatever was to hand – maybe one of those duty-free potatoes.

Perhaps most depressing was the blank rectangle in the middle of the wall, dark in contrast to the rest of it, which had been bleached by the sun. The rectangle was a space where a picture or poster had once hung, maybe something advertising the excitement of going to foreign climes and experiencing the world, adventures about to be embarked upon. The sign was long gone and just the memory of these dreams was all that was left behind. No effort made to replace it, as even the idea of dreaming felt like too much for this tired room.

'Look at this, Alf!' I half whispered. 'What's the point of making a space if you can't be bothered to even try and make it nice?'

'Shhh,' said Alf, half laughing and trying to calm me down. Snobbery about interior decor is seldom endearing, especially when in an overcrowded room. 'We'll be getting on the plane soon.' He soothed me and made me see how ridiculous my furore was, like I somehow need to redecorate every room I find myself in as if I'm a Hollywood diva. I am lucky to be travelling and doing a job I like. I am not Diana Ross or Gemma Collins, am I? And of course, in the scheme of things none of this really matters and there are more important things to worry about in the world, but it didn't stop me from wanting so much more for my fellow passengers!

I calmed down and grabbed my potatoes (not a euphemism). Dad always got excited about Jersey Royals. I was relieved to board the plane.

My serenity was short-lived, however, because arriving back at London Heathrow, my ire was raised yet again when I saw how badly that was designed as well. Terminal 5 too! A relatively new terminal! Rather than being allowed to disembark into the terminal, we were made to get off the plane into the pouring rain and board a bus. For a new airport, surely they could have built enough walkways so everyone could be brought indoors? The airport charabanc drove us to the very far end of the runway to dump us at some kind of small tower where a fire-exit door had been flung open to reveal several flights of stairs towering over us.

The metal of the treads meant there was a constant din of heavy shoes clanging against the steel. Everyone climbed at a slight angle as they tried to use their body to counterbalance the luggage they were forced to haul. On finally gaining access to the airport, the last part of our journey involved walking along a cramped corridor at the top of the immigration hall below. The corridor was like an afterthought, an apology of a space for human beings to creep along like they were hardly there. I pointed it all out to Alf as we went along, which surely must have made me the worst kind of company for another human being.

'Things might have been organised so much better!'

'I know. But look how quickly we're back home!' he soothed me again.

I couldn't shake off this feeling of anger and frustration. I couldn't believe that no one had wanted to make it perfect! Why, though? What was wrong with the world? I hardly wanted to bore Alf with it further. It dawned on me that ignoring my grief, and any feelings at all really, for these first months since Dad died had now manifested as fury at the interior design of an airport. It didn't make any sense.

Friday

Had to go up North – the funeral of a distant cousin of my dad, Norma. It was the first funeral since Dad's. I didn't know her, but Mum needed someone to go with. Funerals are strange occasions when you're not that close to the person who has died; you have less emotional investment in them. People seem to want to make them modern now, but, as I've mentioned, for me they are the one time when tradition comes in quite handy because it tells you what to do when you're so flummoxed you don't know what you're supposed to be doing.

The crematorium was a short distance from the busy main road. Before we got there, we passed a turning for a garden centre and a turning for a hotel offering wedding packages. The buzz of the suburban highway murmured in the background despite the erection of high hedges between the chapel and the road. A car zoomed into the car park like a maniac as we made our way to the chapel. Perhaps they were late for the service, or perhaps they were just trying to drum up more business for the funeral directors.

'Bloody boy racer!' I said to Mum.

A small older woman stepped out of the car and marched ahead of us. We walked through a small garden of remembrance with roses and a pretty model bridge over a trickling river, the sanctity of the space interrupted only by the whirr of a digger in the distance, preparing an extension of the garden, perhaps, or maybe just more graves.

We joined the small group of people assembled at the entrance to the chapel, beneath an arch for mourners to shelter under in case it should rain. To be crying in the rain would be too sad, I suppose, and more like a song. Also the rain plays havoc with my shoulder pads – it would be a double sadness. The hearse began its solemn journey through the car park towards the assembled group. It was preceded in its journey by the funeral director, who had also felt a need to update things, and so while still wearing a traditional morning coat, his trousers were in a bolder stripe than usual, and he wore a bright red waistcoat. His coat had that same red echoed on the lapels. Another reminder of why I, despite my affinity with dressing up and solemn ceremony, should never become an undertaker, because how would I be able to resist seeing a group of people watching and not take it upon myself to put on some kind of performance? The funeral director in his updated version of traditional clothes with his walking cane with the silver knocker on top, to my mind, resembled less of an undertaker and was more like Willy Wonka. I half expected him to do a forward roll and invite us all into the chocolate room.

The speeding woman from the car park – a family friend, I imagined – kept talking throughout the whole of this arrival, commentating on every detail. 'What lovely flowers . . . Doesn't it all look so smart? . . . Gosh, they are strong to take out the coffin like that . . .' which made me wonder if she expected everyone to turn and agree with her. She behaved as if she was watching the ceremony on television. I wondered if she was even aware that she was constantly talking like this. Nervousness, I suppose.

'I don't know why we all wear black, though – it makes it so solemn. I prefer it when people get to wear bright colours. It's a celebration of the life that way!' It was as though this was some sort of tableau, but being presented with the sadness of the occasion in real life, before her own eyes, she was unable to deal with any emotion. Like she somehow needed to fill the silence to avoid confronting her grief.

Continuing with the need to modernise funerals, the celebrant emerged and was perhaps the campest man I had seen since I had looked in the mirror that morning. He walked out of the door with a solemnity that somehow managed to be also flamboyant. I could tell he enjoyed it; it was a part he was playing and he relished it. I knew this because I would be exactly the same. Wearing a white suit and an orange tie, he looked like the Man from Delmonte. He made the sign of the cross at the coffin before inviting everyone to follow it inside.

'He's not even a minister,' the chatty woman behind me muttered, like my own private Huw Edwards narrating the State Opening of Parliament.

'Really?' I murmured.

'Oh no, he's not even religious.' In revelation of this fact, his making the sign of the cross at the start now felt a bit hollow, like he did it just for want of something to do. An empty gesture; he could just as easily have done the Macarena. She continued, 'They pay him two hundred quid and he'll dress up as any denomination you like, any religion, probably.'

'Any religion?'

'So they say.'

'What, even, say, Satanism?'

She shrugged her shoulders and nodded. 'Times are hard.'

The room we filed into resembled less a threshold between this life and the next and more a conference suite, with plain magnolia walls, a large screen at the front, a lectern and chairs arranged neatly in rows; the sort of space a local accountancy firm might hold its quarterly meetings. A door mirroring the one we came in through was apparent at the front – a separate exit for after the ceremony so that a new set of mourners could assemble ahead of their service under the arch we came in through and the owners of the crematorium could maximise the use of the space. An eternal supply of grief.

More alarming was the sign on the wall next to the rows of seats that boldly advised *What to do in the event of a fire*. A confusing statement, since surely that was the reason we were all there.

We shuffled into our seats as the celebrant began taking us on this grief-filled journey.

'Hello, everyone!' he said brightly with a smile. There was a pause. 'I said, *hello, everyone!*'

People fidgeted nervously in their seats, unsure what was expected of them, and then tentatively, they offered up a grumbled, 'He-hello?' in unison.

'That's better! We can't have you all sat there looking like sad little puddings now, can we? For today is about celebrating life! The wonderful life of Jean— sorry, I mean Norma! Don't know where I got Jean from. That's Marilyn Monroe, isn't it?'

It made me grateful we had leant on a traditional ceremony for Dad's funeral. Typically, I had somehow managed to find a way to be superior, even about funerals. The one-man show continued, 'We're joined by Norma's children and her ex-husband, who the children reliably inform me likes to be known as Randy Roger— Oh, sorry, Handy Roger!'

The family laughed along – a moment of release in a day of sadness. 'He's very good, isn't he?' whispered the woman behind me who couldn't stop talking.

The celebrant placed a candle by the side of the coffin on the ledge where the coffin and the flowers had been rested. He lit it with a lighter that he had to fumble around in his pocket to find – an ungainly search deep through his trouser fabric, which made it look like he might also be scratching himself. When he eventually produced the lighter, he looked like he was offering to light someone's fag at a bus stop. I squeezed Mum's hand to make sure she was OK.

After recalling the key moments of Norma's life, the moment of silent reflection descended upon us as we were invited to remember the loved one. It is difficult to recall memories of a person you didn't know, so I looked at the floor and thought about the fact that I had run out of dishwasher salt. In any case, I find these moments of 'silent reflection' tricky because I can't necessarily think about a person on command. In my experience, memories have a tendency to stir in the everyday when you least expect them to, or least *want* them to: the queue at the supermarket, a conversation with a taxi driver or a train full of people. Memories can't be conveniently confined to ceremonies on particular days. Musing on the sanctity of life and the fact that it all must end can seldom be reached in the few minutes allocated while, in this instance, 'The Shoop Shoop Song' played.

As the music's closing bars came to an end, it was time to say goodbye for the final time. Reaching under the lectern awkwardly, the celebrant thumbed around, trying to find a button. He pressed and held it to co-ordinate with his final, 'Ashes to ashes! Dust to dust!' The curtain of synthetic fabric silently began its automated swishy journey to hide the coffin, and in doing so, I think everyone was suddenly on the edge of their seats in anticipation as they saw the curtain about to come to a standstill directly on the naked flame of the candle placed there half an hour before.

Suddenly, the congregation was electrified to think that the whole afternoon was about to go up in flames, thereby witnessing the world's first live cremation played out before our eyes. Scoffing at the fire safety sign on the way in became a cruel irony.

'Oh, better remove this!' The celebrant swooped in with a half-laugh to remove the fire risk just as the curtain was about to cover it. We all breathed a sigh of relief that our lives had been spared. The gratitude for life that we had been struggling to source a few moments before was laid bare for us without realising.

As we exited through the second door, a table stood next to a roll-out banner, and we were invited to make a charity donation. It being modern times when no cash is carried, the charity had thoughtfully placed next to it a card reader, which bleeped as each person paid. The electronic sound as we shook hands with the loved one's family was reminiscent of the checkout area in Morrisons. The conveyor belt of life reaching its bagging area.

'That was a bit close, wasn't it?' said the woman behind as we began our slow procession out into the grey Friday lunchtime light to stand amongst the flowers from other mourners arranged on the floor.

'Yes, it was a bit, wasn't it?'

'I thought the whole place was going to go up! That would have made this a funeral to remember!'

'You know, there's all sorts of ways you can make them memorable now,' I said, attempting more of a full conversation now the ceremony was over and the general milling around was starting. 'Someone I knew had a firework.'

'Where?'

'Come again?'

'Where did he put the firework? Was it inside the body somehow?'

'No, no, that wasn't how he died. It was how we finished the funeral – it went up over London.'

'You put the whole coffin on a firework? It must have rained down a terrible mess.'

'No!' I said, exasperated that I had bothered to start a conversation. 'It was his ashes attached to the firework.'

'Oh, that's jubilant,' she said, staring at the floor imagining the scene, before raising her eyebrows and half smiling as she then walked off through the assembled mourners without acknowledging anyone. She crossed the path and walked up towards the car park, and it dawned on me she didn't have any connection to the funeral at all. She probably just wanted someone to talk to, or just something to do. Something to fill a day.

'You can't please all of the people all of the time'

Dad was always trying to remind me that you can please some of the people all of the time and you can please all of the people some of the time, but you can't please everyone always. And the sooner you realise this the less energy you waste worrying. Or so I've heard.

9

Would you like to meet my mother?

Losing a parent is the moment when you truly become an adult. There are other markers, of course – turning eighteen, living away from home, learning to drive – but none feel as profound as the moment when you realise you no longer have the grown-up protection you had when you were a child. Up until that point, it feels like you could still fall back into childish concerns, tantrums and meltdowns and they would be able to rescue you somehow.

Perhaps it's an odd career choice to be a stand-up comedian when I worry about everything all the time. Perversely, though, it is exactly these petty worries that, in my opinion, draw people to comedy in the first place. No one wants a comic who goes, 'Oh, I am the best person in the whole world and I can't believe how perfect my life is!' People don't go to comedy to see those sorts of people, they go to Instagram.

One such worry is that I always feel like I have broken the law. Whenever I see a headline about a serial killer on the loose, I have a pang that it could somehow be me, even if it's somewhere in another part of the country. I worry that I might have sleep-walked, got in a car or booked a train and got there, committed it and then blithely returned to my bed without realising what I'd done. Sleeping soundly. The atrocities committed in a fugue state.

I think it is unlikely. In my rational mind, I know I haven't done these things, but there is a part of my mind which isn't rational at all. I think there would surely be blood on my pyjamas somewhere, or an axe on the bedside table by the Princess Margaret biography. But maybe somehow it's possible that I might have done these things? After all, I often wake up feeling tired.

I don't know if worrying all the time is connected to growing up gay without being able to talk about it – holding inside something that feels like a terrifying secret that no one should find out about, something other people might think is terrible.

It's not just based on nervousness per se. I worry about everything all of the time. On the few occasions I find myself driving a car, I dread going past people on the pavement for fear that I'll mount the kerb, run them over, somehow without realising, and then speed off, oblivious. To counter this fear as I drive away, I will keep checking my rear-view mirror to make sure they're OK and then, seeing them still walking along perfectly happy, I will check again in the mirror to make sure I'm not just tricking myself into imagining that they are OK. In truth, I check the rear-view mirror so much I am barely looking at the road in front, and so, in reassuring myself that I haven't mown down the people behind me, I risk doing more damage to anyone I am, in fact, driving towards. A metaphor for life, I suppose.

Selfishly, it is less about the fear of knocking someone over and more about the horror of people's reaction. 'How terrible to be a maniac on the road – what must people think?'

The worst advice you can give to a person feeling nervous is 'Oh, don't be nervous', as though they might never have thought about that.

'Good idea! I'll give it a try!'

It's the equivalent of saying, 'Oh, don't be ill!'

'Huh! Thanks, Doc. I hadn't thought of it like that – I guess now I'm cured!'

I was once given the advice that nerves are just the flip side of excitement. Which is good to know and sometimes works, but the little voice in my head has a habit of overriding this by telling me I have no right to even have a go at being a comedian and I am more than likely to fall flat on my face at any minute. However, despite this, I seem to keep throwing myself into situations that make me confront my anxieties.

I once helped my friend, the sports commentator Mark McAdam, report on a football match. It was the Charlton versus Wimbledon game, which was so much fun, especially as the game had loads of goals in it. I never felt like I could get into football, as it always seemed so macho – so serious. I know that football isn't exclusively male, but I always felt like it was mainly men who seemed to be involved when I was growing up.

At Mark's invitation, I was asked to stand on the sidelines to describe what was happening at the game, or, as I believe it is called, 'commentate'. It was for a television programme called *Soccer Saturday,* which I had never heard of, so assumed was just a bit of fun and probably had hardly any viewers anyway. I proceeded not to take it very seriously at all and had a wonderful time throwing myself into flamboyant descriptions of what was happening on the pitch. I had a blast and Mark encouraged me to just be myself – 'Football is for everyone!'

I remarked how one of the players had a shaved head and a beard so looked a bit like me. I told everyone how mean the crowd had been because when one player fell over, the crowd booed. I couldn't imagine falling over and then being taunted for it.

For example, I was once out with a group of highly successful gays, the sort of people who collect art, holiday in Mykonos and wear hats confidently, not in the semi-ironic making-fun-of-myself way that you and I do. We were going to see some trendy theatre piece in a warehouse. I couldn't believe they'd invited me to join them. We had to walk through an underpass, where we found a puddle. Everyone else managed to spring over it like confident gay gazelles – 'gayzelles', if you will. I leapt as best I could, and whilst I might have the wardrobe of Fred Astaire I sadly have the footwork of Fred Dibner and missed my landing, skidded forward, rebalanced myself and fell on my back with my jacket somehow over my head. Amongst these gayzelles I was like Bambi on the ice. They all sort of carried on and mainly pretended it hadn't happened. Though this approach might seem less caring, I would still prefer this option to being booed by hundreds of football fans when falling over. I don't think I'll ever be one of those confident gays, though.

As the goals kept rolling in, the studio kept crossing to us for even more coverage. It was so exciting! I could see why people loved the game. Just when you think it's all over, it can all change. And that tension keeps you so hooked that you forget all your worries and troubles. This was all new to me and I responded accordingly. That is to say I acted like an alien who had just arrived on Earth and had never seen this game 'football' before. I was like a puppy being introduced to a room full of new people. I loved it.

What I hadn't anticipated was that, contrary to my assumption that the show had 'hardly any viewers anyway', the programme has a massive viewership of millions. In the excitement of the game, I hadn't even bothered to check my phone once. When I eventually did, I noticed that my phone had basically melted.

People I hadn't seen for years had sent messages to say they were enjoying it from their local pub, from their phone or from the sofa where they were with their football-loving partner. I felt slightly embarrassed that I had just concentrated on having a fun time, assuming no one even watched the programme. The comments from old friends and even perfect strangers online were very supportive, so I felt like I had done a good job.

However, what I also hadn't anticipated was the response from people on Twitter who weren't so supportive. It would seem that those men who I always thought wouldn't welcome me at the football still didn't. Among lots of very positive, happy comments were reams of people furious that I had been allowed to trespass in their world. They were incandescent about the fact that I was showing off and being silly, not fulfilling what the stereotype of a football pundit should be at all. It was like a punch to the stomach after what had been a really great afternoon.

I think their problem was that I wasn't concentrating on the match in the same way that the other commentators did. I could understand that. It was their time on a Saturday to find out what had happened in the games across the country and this programme was like their sanctuary away from the troubles of the week. And here I was, prancing around, not taking it seriously at all.

It occurred to me that yet again there was a right and a wrong way to behave that was silently acknowledged by everyone going to the football: basically don't be too outlandish or too flamboyant. Hugging, crying, singing or screaming were all permitted but not in a way that was self-aware: the hugs had to be platonic, the crying reluctant and the singing more like shouting. Nothing too refined could be acceptable. In short, I internalised it as a rule that you shouldn't act in a way that would lead people to mark you out as 'gay'. Whatever that meant. However, what I also reasoned with myself was that there actually isn't a right or wrong way to experience football. You could burst into a tap dance or sing Boney M's back catalogue if that was how you wanted to express your jubilation at a goal. There were no rules in the handbook of the game on how you should engage with it, what you should wear or how much experience you should have of the game before you watch it, as long as you aren't causing harm to other people.

It was little wonder that I had never felt comfortable around football games – playing or watching – and that was probably because my way of interacting with the world wasn't welcome there at all. I should point out that Mark along with Stonewall and the team at Sky Sports supported me and stuck up for me completely, and they have worked tirelessly to overturn these attitudes, but there were a few moments that afternoon when there seemed to be a lot of people to overturn.

The angry people on social media seemed to weigh heavy on my mind because they had undone the positivity I'd felt. It was just a bit of fun on a Saturday afternoon as far as I could tell. What was more frustrating was why I checked social media in the first place. It was like I had to look at social media to be reassured that I had done it OK, like I was looking for affirmation.

I think a lot of people do this with social media; it has become a way for us to seek reassurance that we are somehow all right and OK as human beings. It is a place for our opinions to be echoed back at us. I know at its best it gives people a community and a way of reaching out to others who might be sharing an experience, but at its worst, it can be a place that is divisive and hurtful and plays into people's anxieties.

I have an unhappy addiction to poring over negative comments about myself on social media. At my happiest and my most proud, I have often found myself looking for comments from individuals who don't like me. I have obsessed over them and checked their profile and their other tweets and messages. They usually said something about being 'a proud dad' or 'My kids are my life!' or on one occasion, a celebrant who did humanist weddings and funerals felt the need to mention how much they didn't like me – I could only imagine the tone of the life events they would celebrate. All these comments became huge in my brain and played on repeat whenever I was doing anything. I assumed theirs were the opinions of everyone but that most people were too polite to say them to my face. It was like I was being bullied by those girls at primary school again.

The feeling of apprehension about how I might be received only really hung around for the first part of my stand-up career – the first part lasting for around thirteen years. Turning up at far-flung places terrified me because I was scared they would dislike me because of my accent or because I might be too camp or just a bit too weird. I mean, I wasn't up there talking about my wife or my kids. Getting off the plane in cities like Belfast or bouncing off a train in Middlesborough, I would be praying that the audience would be welcoming and in a positive mindset and not so drunk that they would want to shout out. At the Stand in Glasgow or the Glee Club in Birmingham, I would hope that I would do OK so that the show manager's report to the booker would be vaguely positive, and so they would book me again and I wouldn't have to be a failure at the job I had decided I wanted to do.

Often I would go onstage in Middlesborough and be delighted to find that the audience were merry but still up for a good time.

I came to realise that people will mirror what you put out there. So if you look nervous, they will be nervous back at you. If you have confidence, they will feel confident about you and everyone will have a good time. I learnt to affect this eventually, so even if I was absolutely terrified, I would put on the heavy imaginary cloak of confidence, raise my hands up and boom at the audience, 'Are you OK?!' They would respond, 'Yeah!' and the confidence would somehow snowball from there.

In Middlesborough, if it went well, I would treat myself to a Parmo. These food-based treats were a way for me to soothe myself after a gig, especially if I had been feeling nervous and was a long way from home. For the uninitiated, a 'Parmo' is an escalope of chicken, breaded and fried, covered in béchamel sauce and melted cheese with a side of chips, all served in a pizza box. It was always delicious and the best way to end an evening, though perhaps not great for my arteries. It would usually only be available in a chip shop that had disco lights and benches round the side, which might have one person asleep in the corner when you arrived but then a crowd of friends would arrive and suddenly the whole place was turned into a party.

In the worst-case scenarios, the audiences would sort of whimper back and you would know they were never going to like you any way. I would always try to do my best for them, but the nerves would be passed back and forth, the energy decreasing with every pass until I would start rushing and they would be willing me to get off the stage.

Belfast was usually very nice to me, but every time I did a gig there I would end up arriving at the wrong airport – Belfast International. Presumably so called because it is so far away from Belfast that it seems to be in another country. The gig I did a lot there was run by the nicest family. It's been running for years in a high-ceilinged room, a bit like a church, with a high stage to match, so high that you feel like you are on a tight rope.

One night, I started my set, talking about the experience of being gay and living with my parents. A woman in the front row turned her chair around, so she had her back to me. She was clearly drunk. I was feeling confident, or maybe just too tired to be nervous (often the same thing in my experience) – the hours of travel from the airport had clearly worn me out. I decided to ask her why she had done that. 'You all right there? I don't think you're going to get a very good view if you're facing the wrong way . . . ?'

The woman in the front row looked out at the rest of the room with her arms folded. Then she turned around to face me, looking furious. 'My son is worth ten of you!'

I was perplexed. 'But how do you know how much I cost?' I said, trying to seem like I might be a sex worker on the side and also trying to pretend that I was still fun and confident.

She stood up, pointing at me. 'My *son*! He is worth *ten* of you!'

The people around her seemed to be telling her to shut up. I hadn't really said anything offensive. All I could tell was that she was very proud of her son – and what mother isn't? – and that she was furious that I was talking about being gay. I definitely hadn't said anything pejorative about him, nor about anything, really. I have always made a point of talking in the first person because, after all, how can you know what anyone else's experience has been?

She turned to sit back down and abruptly fell off her chair. With that, the whole audience burst out laughing and cheered. I felt sorry for her. She must have thought I was literally not worthy of standing up on stage when her son wasn't on stage – who was ten times better than me. None of it made sense. She was drunk.

No wonder I was anxious when I first started out when I would sometimes get responses like that.

The door staff escorted the lady out, and she was furious. I think it was part of the loop that I was in: desperate for positive affirmation but also fixated on negativity. A group of rugby players were in that night and, very kindly, they took me out afterwards in Belfast and it was so much fun. After my post-gig treat, which that night consisted of chips, they got me absolutely hammered so that I didn't really remember the strange experience with the odd person at the gig, and they proved that despite the negative experiences, there are always more good ones to celebrate than bad.

Worrying what other people think of you is exhausting, especially when things go wrong in confined spaces. I once boarded a long-haul British Airways plane and found myself sat on the end of a central row of seats. The two members of cabin crew were from 'the old school'. He had a moustache, and she had the strongest chignon bun I had ever seen. They were what I imagined were called 'Legacy Contract Staff': trained in the job when flying was still glamorous and flight attendants strode confidently through airports wearing hats while the likes of Joan Collins and Michael Winner could still be glimpsed waiting to get on Concorde.

They carried with them a certain authority that suggested they would be good in a crisis. They had been trained in 'service with a half-smile'. Their management were known as CSDs – which stood for Cabin Service Directors or, colloquially, 'C***s Standing at the Door'. On-board announcements were always in clipped accents and concluded with a smart 'We wish you a pleasant flight and a very good afternoon'. They belonged to a bygone era in many ways, but I loved them. They even had their own accent – it involved using more 'ya' sounds. So 'Welcome aboard British Airways' sounded like 'Wyelcyome Aboard Briyatysh Ayrweeys.'

I nodded a hello to my seat mates as we all sat down. There were three women in their fifties sharing the row of seats next to me, who seemed pleasant if nervous and vaguely annoyed as they rammed their holdalls into the crowded overhead lockers. Perhaps most bizarre was their choice of outfits. They had all worn white linen – surely the worst possible colour for travel – made into blouses and wide-lapelled blazers. They looked like they were attending a Diane-Keaton-in-a-Nora-Ephron-film convention.

The cabin crew performed their safety demonstration, rolling their eyes as they did it, sarcastically tying up their life jackets and blowing into the whistle like they were auditioning to be in a new stage version of *Anything Goes*. They were fantastic. My seat companions were less amused and audibly tutted and shook their heads vigorously at the mention of any kind of in-flight emergency, erasing the image of a disaster from their minds. They all gripped each other's hands as the plane took off and then breathed heavy sighs of relief once we were airborne.

The drinks service soon began and the posh cabin crew were beside us. 'Wyould ya lyike a dryank?' they asked. I opted for a red wine. The other three went for sodas with lime.

The steward poured me a glass and placed it on the fold-down table. Getting into the spirit of the flight, I reached down to browse the in-flight magazine but, in doing so, nudged the table and somehow sent the cup flying onto the woman next to me's white blouse. The red liquid caused a horrible stain as the small plastic cup tumbled to the floor.

'Oh, I'm so sorry!'

The woman glanced down. 'Oh no!' she said, distraught and immediately showing the other ladies in the row. 'OH

NOOOOOO!' They all looked panicked, and stood up to let her out of the seat before they all accompanied her to the tiny toilet.

Another lady across the aisle leant over – she could see how alarmed I was. I was both panicked and devastated. 'What happened?' she asked calmly.

'It was my wine! I didn't mean to! It just tripped and spilled on her blouse!'

'Ahh, I see, that's what it was. It's OK. I'm sure it'll come out.'

'Oh gosh, I am SO sorry!' I said in the direction of the stressed people.

'Don't worry,' said the woman across the aisle, leaning back in her seat. 'I'm sure it will come out.' Though the more she repeated it, the less I believed it.

'What's hyappyened?!' said the stewardess, marching up to the toilet. 'Has thyere beeen an emergencya??'

'The man!' said one of the woman's friends. 'He spilled wine on her blouse!'

'Club syodarrr! Immediatelya,' shouted the stewardess frantically. 'Here, try this. It shyould weerryk!' not sounding like it would work at all.

'If I could take it to a dry cleaner's – or buy her a new one – I would do it right now. I am just so sorry!' I said to the lady across the aisle.

I was distraught. The anxious voice in my head was loud now and I could feel myself wanting to run away from the situation, but there was nowhere I could go to hide. It felt like everyone on the airplane was staring at me. I had to leave my seat and pace around in the tiny galley kitchen at the back and speak to someone. Anyone! The stewardess returned with empty cans of club soda.

'Are yar eeekay?' she asked me kindly, returning to get more cans. 'What hyappened?'

'I splashed red wine on the lady's outfit!'

'Oh nyoooooo!'

The steward who had served me the wine earlier entered the galley.

'Hey, guess what!' she said to him. 'This gentleman only went and spilled wine on the lady's clyothes!'

'Eoh neo! Thyat's turrible,' he said, bursting out laughing at the awfulness of it all.

'What can I buy them? To say sorry. There must be something! I can hardly get them a drink to say sorry! What would you like in this circumstance?'

'Dyon't beat yoursyelf up. Eiam sure thyere is somethang in the dutee-fra catalyogue,' he said.

'What about perfume?' I asked imploringly.

'No!' said the stewardess. 'The main thing that perfume is made of . . . is alcohol!' before barely suppressing more laughter.

I slumped back into my seat, next to the other ladies who had returned from helping their companion. There was obviously nothing more they, or anyone, could do. They all seemed to be angrily staring at the seats in front. I tried to avoid making eye contact.

The stained-blouse woman returned to her seat, wearing a British Airways tabard as a replacement.

'I'll hyang it up een the fryunt,' said the stewardess who had composed herself and was actually doing an excellent job of diffusing the tension. 'Don't worry – you can barely see the stain now.'

We sat there in awkward silence, staring straight ahead at the in-flight entertainment screens neither of us had even had a chance to start watching. I certainly didn't feel like experiencing the promised options of music, films, TV, and even computer games!

The lady whose shirt I had so clumsily ruined turned to me, and as she did so, I turned and said, 'I am so—' but she had already started speaking.

'Sorry if—'

I was even getting my apology wrong. 'Sorry, you go first.'

'No, after you.'

'No, really, please, after you . . .'

'I was just going to say I am sorry if I screamed and made a fuss then.'

'I am *so* sorry – I can't believe it's happened. If there's anything I can do – if I could take it to a dry cleaner's, I would!'

I crept out to the kitchen galley, my only refuge, and explained that I needed to buy something from duty-free, immediately. Flicking through the brochure, there was a small locket that had some kind of purple stone in it. I wasn't sure if it was hideous or not but it was the only thing that wasn't perfume or a phone charger. A phone charger hardly seemed like the best way to say sorry.

'It's nice! She'll love it!' said the steward, still smirking through his moustache. He clearly thought it was hideous. Walking back, I presented it to my seat-mate.

'Oh, you didn't need to do this!' she said, not meaning it. 'Ah, wow, it's beautiful,' she said, also not meaning it.

'It's the best they had!' I said, trying not to sound like I was giving an apology for my apology gift.

We all smiled at one another and shrugged. There then followed an awkwardness as we all turned together to put our earphones in and watch the in-flight entertainment, silently, all of us trying to ignore the moments before, exhausted from the pressure and pretending so hard that none of it had ever even happened. Dad would have been able to tackle all of this head on; he would have said sorry in a confident, friendly way and made the whole thing go away. He wouldn't have panicked. He wouldn't have worried. In that awkward silence that I found myself in I reflected on this, and then worried some more.

I have always tried to challenge myself with the gigs that I have done. I think it's based on feeling that I must always work hard to prove myself in the entertainment industry. After all, I get to do fun things, so the least I can do is make sure I give it my all. On some level, I have always wanted to prove myself to my dad. I think in some ways he would have preferred me to use my A-levels to do something stable and secure, though I think he would eventually admit that in this world, there is little security anyway. Nonetheless, I wanted to show to him that I could earn a living working in 'showbiz'.

In the late 2000s I was offered a series of gigs in the Middle East. This marked a considerable step change in terms of my feelings of security. Given that the Middle East was not known for being positive towards LGBTQ+ people, and in certain countries had laws that punished it often very severely, it was at best brave and at worst reckless of me to think I could just mooch out there and do a few shows. My aim was always to prove that I could gig anywhere. And also I needed the money.

My experience of the Middle East was very different to what I had expected in lots of ways. It made me ashamed to think of what a limited understanding we have in Western Europe of other cultures. Even for me to talk about 'the Middle East' is ridiculous, as I am, of course, only talking about the area that I visited. Ahead of the gigs I was doing, I was met at the airport by Tania, an English woman who had lived there for two years and who was helping Gordon, also at the airport, who was putting on the gigs in the hotel.

Tania was friendly and posh and drove really fast in the Mercedes they used for picking up comics for the gigs. As we drove through the city, I was surprised to see there were actually a large number of gay couples walking around. They seemed so carefree in their hand-holding and the warm way men greeted one another. It was like being in Barcelona or New York.

Then it was explained to me by Gordon, turning round from the front seat of the Mercedes. 'No, no – Arab men often walk along holding hands if they are friends. They aren't lovers!'

I obviously would wish for the gay people there to have freedom but I also felt a sadness that we culturally didn't have the same attitude towards men generally showing affection to one another.

I was apprehensive about the gig that night. There were three comics on the bill from all around the world; one from the Netherlands, one from Australia and me. It was taking place in the function room of a local hotel, which was large and apparently sold out.

'But, Gordon, I'm just so scared – won't they dislike me for being gay? I mean, will I get into trouble for just being gay, never mind talking about it on stage?'

'No, no, Tom, you will only get in trouble if you promote homosexuality.'

'Yes, but just me being gay on stage, couldn't that constitute promotion of it in some way? People might see me and be inspired?'

Gordon looked at me with a wry smile. 'The way you do it? No, darling.'

'I think you'll be fine,' piped in the Dutch comic. 'Gordon, is it a problem to do political humour?'

'Well, it depends. If you are making fun of European politics, then that's fine.'

'Yes, that's what I'm doing.'

'You just can't make fun of the king or the political system here – you won't get beheaded or anything, but the audience will just feel . . .'

'Afraid?'

'No, just uncomfortable.'

'So, Gordon, they don't want insurrection?' I chimed in to try and chill everyone out.

'Insurrection? As I said before, the way you do it, no, darling.'

The gig was fine. Good, even. There was a mix of local people and people from around the world, as well as Americans working in the local oil industry. Everyone was very nice.

All three of us comics breathed a sigh of relief. Gordon was delighted, and he and Tania immediately started to dismantle the stage and the banners on either side ready for our show the next night at another hotel.

Walking through the grand marble lobby, the Dutch comic said he was going to bed, while the Australian said she was meeting a friend. 'He's the son of a billionaire and a very powerful guy here – I've known him for years. Look, Tom, I'd invite you to join us but he's very strict and he can't be seen to be around any gay people. It would be bad for his family.'

'Really?'

'Oh, yes.'

'And you still want to meet this guy?'

'He's a billionaire! Hell, yes! Oh, jeez, he's over there – if you say hello, just don't mention being gay or anything like that, OK?'

I hadn't felt in any way uncomfortable until this point. Near the door, her stocky, camp friend was waiting for us. He certainly didn't look very grand. He greeted the Australian friend with a hug. She then reluctantly introduced me before I could get away. 'This is Tom – he's one of the other comics.'

'Oh, hellloo!' he said boldly in an American accent – the trait of the international rich, making it impossible to know where they are from. He offered out his hand. 'We'll stay here for drinks, right?'

'Sure, whatever you like, sure,' said the Australian. 'I thought you wanted to go out for dinner, but whatever, sure.'

We found a table in the small bar on the first floor and began chatting. Being a people-pleaser, I felt like I had to stay to try and make him like me.

'Good show, then?'

'Sure, yes,' I said, trying to read him. 'Much nicer than we expected in a way – well, we didn't know what to expect, really.'

'I see. British people,' he said, leaning in my direction, 'they're not well liked here. A lot of my friends, they hate you.'

'Me?' I asked.

'No, not you specifically, just British people. But I'm glad you were well liked. It's good to see you again,' he said to the Australian awkwardly. A silence followed. 'Hey, did I tell you I got a kestrel?'

'What? No way!' screeched the Australian excitedly.

He produced his phone as if to show a photograph of it. Instead, it was a video. 'Here she is – I feed her myself.' The video showed him cross-legged on the floor, the bird walking around in front of him while he held a mouse out and laid it on the floor. The kestrel picked it up with its beak and then gored it with its claws. All the time he was laughing delightedly. It was absolutely horrible to watch, with blood going all over the floor. 'Pretty cool, right?'

'Right,' I said, harrowed.

'Pretty neat, wow,' said the Australian.

Reeling a bit, I said, 'I'll get us some more drinks – same again?'

'Sure, thanks,' said the man. I was keen to let them have their catching-up time. Despite his horrifying bird-feeding video, he seemed pretty happy to talk to me. Standing at the bar, I could hear their conversation: 'I don't mind them – he seems nice – I just don't like the public displays of it – why do they have to have marches and make a big song and dance about things?'

'Oh, well, I don't like any public displays of affection – not from anyone!' said the Australian.

I was really chilled to the bone, especially because I knew I couldn't really say anything. I had, after all, come to a place where I knew I wouldn't have the same legal protections, and attitudes would be different. I did feel hurt that the Australian hadn't stuck up for me, though.

'Here we are!' I said, flamboyantly placing the drinks down. I was angry but had the nagging feeling that in this location, I had no grounds to defend myself other than to try to be a nice person. A decent person. I could hardly tell him off.

Gordon texted me to say he had finished packing up the stage equipment and would I like to join him and Tania for a drink. I made my excuses and left the Australian and the billionaire to their drinks and skipped back to the lobby to meet Gordon.

'Now, I know you were worried about being gay here but actually there is a place I can take you to – it's quite secret, but I think it'll be OK.'

'Where is it?'

'It's a gay bar! It should be kicking off now . . .' he said, pulling back his sleeve to check his watch as we walked out of the hotel's front door and carrying the stage banners under his arm.

'Brenda's!' he announced when we were in the car. 'It's called Brenda's.' Gordon craned round from the front seat. Tania was concentrating on enjoying driving really fast.

The bar was situated in the basement of a hotel where the elaborate blue-tiled lobby doubled as a flower shop. I suppose some people might say this was a giveaway in many ways. I followed Gordon and Tania past the front desk and along a side corridor to where the kitchen was. We walked almost into the kitchen but took a small door on the left. I was apprehensive, but at the same time very intrigued.

Gordon opened it and we headed down a flight of stairs to another door, which we opened and, on going through it, suddenly found we were there at the promised bar – a hot, dark basement space with live music and dancing. The stage was right next to the door so that as you arrived, you were basically on stage with the band, an Afrobeat group playing loudly. As soon as I stepped through the door, it was like a party and stepping down off the stage into the bar made you feel like you were a Hollywood star making a grand arrival at the Oscars.

'See!' said Gordon 'I told you it was a much more welcoming place than people realise!'

The room was filled with people from all over the world, alongside Arab men and even American service personnel. A sign graced the wall behind the bar: '*No touching and no men dancing with men!*' which seemed to be adhered to. People walked around the dance floor selling scarves for men to drape around the men they were dancing with without actually touching. People made it work. Though with so many people throwing scarves around each other, it did feel even more camp than it would have been if people had just been allowed to dance without them.

It was not as free as my experiences had been in London, but I was impressed that the owners had made it happen. We stayed for a while and enjoyed the drinks. There was an even darker section at the back of the room, but Gordon said we shouldn't go over there, which made me even more curious.

After the trepidation I had felt about the gig the previous night, the following night I was feeling much more relaxed. We all arrived at the new venue to do our set and were suddenly greeted by the Australian's billionaire friend.

'Oh, he had such a great time last night,' whispered the Australian.

He came bounding over to me. 'Thank you so much for the drinks! It was so great to meet you. I checked out some of your stuff online and it's really good.'

I was very taken aback. 'Oh, thank you.'

'Hey, would you like to meet my mother?'

This friendship had really escalated quickly. He minced over to his mother, who was actually a friendly, camp American woman wearing big glasses and a cardigan. 'Oh, he's been going ON and ON about what a great time he had last night!'

'Really?'

'Sure has, honey! Have you enjoyed your trip?'

'Oh yes, very much, thank you.'

'It's a great town, right? Full of surprises!'

'Yes, indeed.' And, indeed, it certainly was.

If people don't like you, it's OK. You can't please all of the people all of the time, but if you hide yourself away for fear of other people's opinions, you might never go anywhere. Sometimes when you please yourself, the people who liked you already end up liking you even more, and those who didn't might just be convinced otherwise. And while that might be shallow, it can feel fantastic.

'Bastards!'

Dad would shout this about people if they revealed themselves to be bastards. He didn't mean it, though; he said it mockingly. I think it was his way of laughing at the bad things in the world.

10

The sea, Tom! It's too loud!

I met my dad in a gay bar in Soho. I was in my late twenties. He didn't know it was a gay bar, and to be honest, neither did I. 'This is a real old-fashioned man's pub, isn't it?' he said enthusiastically. He was excited that in a world of self-conscious media types, he had managed to find London's last proper boozer. It was a pub where men, older men, with shaved heads or bald heads, and gruff looks on their faces, could sit at the bar or at a table and make conversation with one another. They looked just like Dad really, though Dad was in his white shirt from work and not a tank top.

'Dad, I think it's a gay bar.'

'Is it?! Oh well, they did seem friendly.' I looked up at the huge rainbow flag above the fireplace and worried about him. We'd arranged to meet in town for lunch because I had a work meeting and he had a meeting about coaches. I wish I'd paid more attention to what it was.

I think there comes a point when every child worries about their parents. It dawns on them that they might know more than their parents about how the world is now, how it really is, and they fear their parents might have been left behind. The parent, of course, feels exactly the same in reverse and continues to worry about the child in the way they always have, knowing that the child thinks they know more than them. The parents know they don't; they never can because they don't have the perspective of age. Essentially, we all think we know what life is about but the truth is, life is probably more about realising we're only here for such a short time.

My dad and I were very different at times. Dad was born during the Second World War, when people had to get on with things because there wasn't much to go round, your food was rationed and you didn't know how long you had before more bombs started to land. I suppose as a result, it must have been a time of more rules and regulations, and thus it would have been a more disciplined world. Dad would tell me how it used to be a criminal offence to have a public clock showing the incorrect time. He just missed National Service, but he was from a time still shrouded in militaristic tones because after two world wars, it had to be. As a result, Dad was punctual, organised and efficient. Never prone to writing more than he had to. On Christmas presents, his gift tags would read *TO TOM*. When I picked him up on this, we all laughed, but he seemed confused. 'Well, that is who it's for!'

I, on the other hand, have always been creative, flouncy, oversensitive and, because I am all of these things, seldom punctual. It takes a lot of time to work out what pocket square matches my tie (but without looking like it matches too much); it takes a lot of time to work out how I feel when I read some often highly emotional Instagram post about *RuPaul's Drag Race*; it takes time to read my cookery books and make their elaborate recipes and recreate their artful photographs.

Whereas Dad was brought up with rationing and bomb sites, I was brought up with the emergence of Eurostar and café culture coming to the UK. We had Patisserie Valerie on the high street, coffee suddenly came with froth on top and food was inspired by flavours from around the world. Life was becoming something that could be curated, lived self-consciously in a series of vignettes and montages, which we'd plan in advance; trips to far-flung places were replete with photoshoots for the sole purpose of being uploaded onto social media for other people's approval.

For my millennial self, there was always time and space to make things perfect. The vibe was everything! Every moment had to be pondered to work out how I was feeling about said vibe. Dad, on the other hand, would turn on the big light in the middle of the ceiling. I would gasp like a fish just taken out of the river and immediately run around the room switching on the lamps, cursing that I had been born into a family without dimmer switches. I think Dad's attitude was that the main light afforded us the best light, so why wouldn't we use it? It was as though he had never even read *World of Interiors* or studied the Soho House book about amber lighting states to unwind in.

To my mind, dinner was something to be languid about and could be served lukewarm from a central serving dish or tagine. Whereas Dad's priority was to serve food hot to prove that it had been freshly cooked and also to warm you up if you had been outside in the cold London air for a long time.

I have always been about performance and showing off. Dad was always about practicality and getting things done. For this reason, I think we could sometimes wind each other up.

He would know better than me and I would know better than him. '*All right!* Do it your way! You know everything!' he'd gasp if I ever questioned his authority on driving routes or how to pack away the garden furniture. He wanted to do his best for me, I realise this now, but we disconnected sometimes and it drove both of us to distraction because deep down inside, I always wanted to prove to him that I was an adult, even if I didn't always behave like one. I would hate for him to seem grumpy, though. He may have been born at a different time to me, but he was always open-minded and positive about things, open to discussion, open to new experiences; he loved people, and he loved doing the right thing by people. I think it was just my constant need to change things that probably drove him, at times, to distraction, and frankly, who could blame him?

Is your family blessed with a camp child? If you have been entrusted with one of these God-given miracles, like an angel descended on your home life out of nowhere, you might have been treated to various performances throughout your shared life. In the case of my family, they had the pleasure of watching long-winded 'plays' performed from behind the curtains (the ones with the tie-backs were my particular favourites, as they most resembled an actual theatre). These spontaneous theatrical productions must have driven my parents mad with boredom as I went into tremendous detail recalling every moment of our recent trip to the new Tesco that had opened on the Sidcup bypass. They laughed, generously, as I liberally used my new favourite word 'actually', sometimes several times per sentence:

'The man at the trolleys was actually very nice, though he did say we would need to actually bring it back afterwards, actually.'

Suspense was everything, and I would keep everyone waiting for a long time, having made them arrange their seats in proper order, with 'children' (at this point just my younger brother) sat on a cushion on the floor. I would then use my time wedged between the curtain and the window to 'rehearse' the inaugural performance of *Tesco, Actually*.

Though these flamboyant theatrical productions might have entertained my grandmother for a short while, they couldn't last for too long. In my later childhood, through my teen years, and up to this point, my thirties, the plays became more focused on interiors and how my parents should rearrange their kitchen. I decided for my eighteenth birthday that they should redecorate the lounge in white and brushed steel with lots of palm plants. It was a theme that I am sure Carol Smillie on *Changing Rooms* (the number one show at the time) would be proud of – minimalist and modern yet still homely, and more importantly, still available in IKEA. My parents were pleased with the result, though why they didn't tell me to shut up, I don't know.

I think perhaps it came down to my mother's inbuilt sense of making sure we were keeping up with the other people in suburbia. With this new modern palette of 'white/plant green/ metal' we might have created a house that looked like a storage room in a garden centre, but it was so modern that we could look down our noses at anyone who was still clinging to the chintz cushions, patterned carpets and curtains with tie-backs that people loved from before.

Later, 'the way we eat' became my new improving project. What a gift for them! Some people would pay thousands for a lifestyle guru or a mental health professional to help them make sense of their lives, but my parents had someone right there to do it all for them – what luck! Admittedly, when I was living with them, I had never had a discernible career except lots of gigs, and yes, I had never had my own home so still didn't really understand how council tax and bins worked, I didn't have a pension or an income that was anywhere near the national average – but I had such insight from all those fancy design magazines I kept buying and those modern art galleries I kept visiting (or at least went to sit in the coffee shops of). I had so much more insight than they could ever dream of, and here I was, able to visit all my wisdom on their lives in suburban Bromley!

Salads would no longer be shredded leaves with tomato and cucumber on top – we would now have a 'Wedge Salad', where you had a wedge of iceberg lettuce with the dressing and the other bits drizzled on top. 'How do I eat this?' my dad would plead.

'However you like!' I said excitedly and unhelpfully.

Potatoes didn't need to be the staple of every meal – we could have healthy quinoa and bulgur wheat. 'But we're hungry, Tom!'

I once decided that I should make my parents a risotto from scratch. I could be just like Nigel Slater, stirring the homemade chicken stock into the little pearls of risotto rice, ladle by ladle, while my mind mused on the world before we would all sit down and eat this wholesome meal together like characters in a film.

What I had failed to take into account was that the posh risotto rice I had bought needed to be soaked overnight to remove the hard outer husks. I rinsed them for a bit and just started making the risotto according to Nigel's simple but oh-so-wholesome recipe. I ladled and I stirred and I mused for the forty-five minutes as per the instructions. The rice was still hard, though. So I kept stirring and ladling. In the end, I had to make more stock but rather than from scratch, I did it with Bisto. It wasn't the same at all. I kept on stirring, but still the stock didn't make a difference.

'Is it nearly ready? I think your dad is getting a bit hungry . . . ?' Mum said gently. 'It's just that it is twenty-five to ten now and, well, we usually eat around five or six.'

I served it up, complete with a sprinkling of parsley and a flourish of grated Parmesan, and proudly placed it down in

Mum's new serving bowls, which I had decided could double up as risotto receptacles. The rice wasn't cooked. It was hard. Like ball bearings. We crunched our way through the risotto as best we could, the ten o'clock news playing in the background. It should have been so perfect, but it wasn't.

'It's nice, Tom! Very nice,' said Dad, crushing another grain of rice.

'Oh yes, very tasty,' said Mum, positively.

I made them cheese on toast as a 'snack' but which we all knew was the actual meal.

Despite living in their house as this precocious lodger, my parents, exhausted, did let my rules like 'No Pyrex on the table' come into force. On the television, people were always placing things in serving dishes with herbs scattered on top. It seemed so elegant, so refined. I was desperate to make us just like this. White serving dishes became part of the order of things. They didn't make anything taste better; if anything, it just added to the drama by making us decant things into serving dishes right before dinner, and then increase the washing up afterwards, but for some reason, my parents put up with it and they put up with me.

We once had beef about beef. Mum had cooked Sunday lunch, but I considered myself to be an expert in culinary skill because I used to do shifts in my friend's dad's restaurant and because I had watched a lot of *Ready Steady Cook* (the Fern Britton and Ainsley Harriet eras).

There was a clear division in our family about how beef should be cooked. Mum liked it medium, and so did I. Dad on the other hand liked it well done. I think it was about mistrusting anything that wasn't cooked 'properly'. My brother didn't mind and generally avoided arguments. Mum had cooked the Sunday beef to perfection; it was pink in the middle and well done at the ends. Though my mum considers herself to be not very confident in the kitchen, she is actually very good. 'Mum, this looks amazing!' I said and Mum beamed. It was a great day. Dad performed his master-of-the-house role and dutifully carved the meat, slicing it onto an oval serving plate (it was an old plate that my parents didn't use but which I had decided was 'so chic!'). Having completed the task, he then put the slices back into the oven to 'keep warm'.

Taking them out again when the Yorkshire puddings had risen magnificently, the beef had gone from medium to well done. 'Dad!' I exclaimed.

'What?' said my mum, turning from the oven with the baking tray, her glasses steamed up from facing the intense heat.

'It's the same, it's only a bit more well done,' said Dad.

'It's overcooked! The meat was perfect before, but now it's overcooked! Dad! Why did you put it back in?'

'What difference does it make?'

'Because now it's overcooked!' I said, agitated.

'Tom . . .' said Mum, as if to say, 'Leave it . . .'

'Oh, I can't do anything right!' said Dad in a huff, holding a colander in one hand, about to plate up the broccoli florets.

'You can, but I don't understand why you would be obsessed with not wanting things to be medium rare!'

'It has to go back in because I didn't want it to get cold,' he said in a voice that suggested he was talking to a child. 'I suppose you want us to have a dinner that's cold, do you?'

'No, I just don't want it to be overcooked!'

'Tom!' said Mum again.

'Oh, fine. Have it your way!' And with that, he threw the colander across the room and left the kitchen, grabbed his car keys and left the house. We didn't know where he went.

Mum, my brother and I sat and ate the roast beef in silence. 'You had to wind him up, didn't you?' said Mum, coldly, in contrast to the beef. I hadn't meant to. I just wanted to help make things better. It was like this mist came over me and I just had to express how I felt, no matter how trivial. I think he saw it as an assault on him as a person. The trouble with parents and children is that from the perspective of the child, parents aren't people, they are super humans able to take anything. However, my dad was a normal person who had an ego and sensitivities that I couldn't see – I just thought he was a rock to stand on so I could see further. I thought he could take anything.

He was much more emotional than he thought he was, he just didn't express it as 'emotion' as we would term it now. I dare say it happens to all of us as we get older and realise we have so little agency over the world we live in. Things seem so frustrating, especially when you know there is a better way of doing things but no one listens to you. Both Dad and I liked our own approaches, and he just showed his frustration with my stubbornness outwardly. But he could also show others short shrift, especially when he thought they weren't doing the right thing. Ultimately, he wanted to make things right. He had a big sense of what's fair.

He once called a traffic warden an unrepeatable word. He wasn't even getting a ticket, he just hated traffic wardens so intensely. And it wasn't to the warden's face – Dad was sat next to me in the car.

It wasn't without good cause. Along with his highly developed sense of good behaviour, he always had a sense of what is right and just. In the case of the traffic warden, he would admit it was unfair to speak like that about someone who was just trying to do their job, but also he would be quick to retort, 'It's not very fair when they issue coach drivers with a fine – sometimes when they've not done anything wrong!'

Dad worked as a coach driver for most of his life and so had spent a lot of his time railing against the tickets issued to him and his drivers for staying more than a few seconds in a yellow box, often just because a car somewhere in front had suddenly stopped and caused an unexpected hold-up. 'Sixty-five quid those *bastards* at the council want to take off a driver! That's a day's wages after tax!'

Sometimes, they'd be issued by a traffic warden despite the driver parking within the rules – the ticket would be incorrectly issued regardless, in the hope that the driver would pay it because it was too much work to appeal it. It was my privileged and protected life that had me say to Dad, 'You shouldn't get angry at him! If you've got a problem, you should speak to the local MP or the council – it's so uncivilised!' I must have sounded ridiculous to him with my simplistic view of the world, like I had learnt how things work from a cartoon and from spending too much time with people who'd spent their whole life working in the arts. Which basically I had.

'Them bastard traffic wardens are on commission and the councils make millions from it – they don't care! They're arseholes!'

Whether or not this was true, I don't know, but it was Dad's heightened sense of injustice that seemed to inflame him. It was like one wrong formed part of a whole world in which injustices big and small snowballed to make people too weary to question it. 'Sixty-five quid might not seem a lot to some toffee-nosed bloke in the city, but to a coach driver, who might be trying to support a family on that . . . and then out of nowhere, that's it – gone!'

He would be incandescent – exasperated – that no one on high had thought about how rules affect real people, no one acknowledged the complexity of the world and no one seemed to care about working people just trying to get through the day.

Sat around the kitchen table at the end of the day over dinner, Dad would rant against these cruel truths as Mum rolled her eyes and I became more depressed at the state of the world.

'Bastards!' Dad would shout about people who'd fallen foul of his judgement. Sometimes he said it jokingly, sometimes with the sense that it was almost overwhelming him. It was born out of care for the people around him and a despair that the world could be so devoid of empathy. Of course, even this is a simplistic rendering, but I think it was the fact that the complexity of a situation wasn't considered, that a politician, traffic warden or council official hadn't put themselves in someone else's shoes that he found so galling. It's a complicated set of circumstances to understand, but the world is complicated.

When I was last on tour, I booked a hotel for my tour manager and I to stay in during my Cornwall dates. He'd been putting up with me for months on tour, so I felt like he deserved the best. However, he had made a mistake with his diary and it turned out that he couldn't make those dates, and suddenly, my plans were thrown into disarray. I thought I could get the train down to the tour venue and get taxis around. Then the night before, the weather changed and Great Western Railway cancelled most of their trains heading to the South-west in case the high winds caused a tree to fall on the line or flooding threatened the railway line near the sea.

I mentioned it to Dad, and he immediately offered to drive me – he was like this, always quick to help; nothing was ever too much for him. Mum said she would come as well. It would be a family trip and they could enjoy the fancy hotel too! It was perfect, and it felt like the sort of thing I would love to share with my parents to prove that I was not only a good son but also a fully fledged adult who could book hotel rooms for them!

Since I would be leaving them to continue my tour after Cornwall, I had rather nervously arranged to collect a hire car in St Austell and drive myself to the hotel with Mum and Dad following behind in the Ford Fiesta Finesse. I didn't want to do the whole drive on my own, as I had only recently passed my driving test, and also I am a terrible driver. The Ford Fiesta Finesse was a practical car, but it wasn't glamorous: burgundy red – or more accurately, brown – it had moss on the back window and a propensity to squeak when it braked. It sounded a bit like all the screaming souls of hell, which certainly added to the drama.

Dad let me drive the last part of the journey to warm me up for when I got the hire car. Going through the steep inclines of Devon in the pouring rain, I think it took a lot of will power for Dad not to echo the brakes and scream at me when I found myself having to take the car down into first gear to grumble our way along, the car now sounding like it was crying out in pain, like a man who had just had his leg run over. (For the record, even with my bad driving, I didn't run anyone over.)

Once we had separated at the car hire place, the sun started to come out and we set off, me cautiously in front, with only the satnav to keep me company. I drove along the winding roads of Cornwall, feeling quite confident about my driving. I stuck to the speed limit religiously, for fear of a police stop or a speed camera I couldn't see. White vans angrily overtook me, and four-wheel drives glowered as they pulled up to the hire car's bumper like angry Grace Jones fans. I wanted to wind down the window as they passed and shout, 'There is a speed limit, you know? Is it just a joke to you? Is it optional? Because maybe if it's all optional, we can all just do whatever we like, hmm?' But, of course, if I had done, they would have driven past long before I could have said it, and it would have been so distracting I probably would have driven the car into a drystone wall.

The hotel I had booked was beautiful, tucked along a row of houses by the side of a cove. The turn-off was secreted away at the end, where a short driveway led to an unassuming entrance and covered car park. Once I had parked – which took me ages, in case I was too far outside of the white lines and would be arrested by the traffic police – I walked into the hotel. Immediately, I was greeted by a beaming man with a clipboard while another staff member took my bags to my room without me even saying anything. I could barely look at the handsome man with the strong eyebrows (a sign of good genes, surely?) who had greeted me because I was so distracted by the incredible view through the plate-glass window opposite the door. The sea stretched on forever. The hotel was so thoughtfully designed that they didn't even need a reception desk; it was modern, minimalist and it had new ways of doing things. I thought it really was amazing.

Everywhere I looked was another impeccably thought-out view. From the main atrium I found myself in, a sculpture graced one corner, a water feature underlined the view straight in front while a fireplace burned away the autumn chill on my left. Along with the bold, confident swathes of red, crimson and pink on the wall, the whole space was amazing.

I was taken to my room along from the yoga studio and the juicing station. Someone walked past me in dance pants, and I wondered if I was either in a religious cult or in dance school (some people would say these are the same thing). 'The hot tubs are available for use, so just let us know and we'll make sure one is reserved for you.' It was music to my ears to know I could reserve a hot tub on the cliff top, just like a table at a restaurant! Would they serve bread rolls too? I hoped so.

Our identical rooms would be next to each other. The beds faced the windows, so you had an uninterrupted view across the balcony, the beach and the ocean beyond.

It was while I was enjoying the view that I became slightly concerned about the whereabouts of my parents. I sat getting anxious in the reception area, again gazing out at the Atlantic, watching as a storm seemed to be coming in. But then someone offered me a smoothie, and I was calm again.

Suddenly, I felt a change in the air.

My parents had arrived, soaked. 'There you are. Haven't you checked your phone?!' The truth was, I hadn't checked my phone at all because I had been so relaxed. Also, the remoteness of the hotel meant that there was no phone reception and I had not bothered to join the Wi-Fi.

My parents wheeled in their case while carrying coats and a holdall of other things. The sorts of things my mum would insist they brought just in case they needed them. Walking boots were carried in a bag for life, even though they were seldom needed. Jackets were piled up over arms and a bag carried the water and sandwiches bought en route.

The strongly browed man approached Dad with a friendly beam. 'Good afternoon, sir. Can I take your bags?'

'No, you can't!'

'Would you like a drink?' he asked, because surely that is the first thing weary travellers would want rather than dealing with check-in admin.

'No, I would not! We just want to check in.'

'Well, actually, Dad, they don't have a reception here, they just do it—'

'Didn't you even look at your phone?'

'No, Dad, I was just getting settled here—'

'We didn't have the address for the hotel! We've been trying to find it but there's no phone reception.'

'We got really lost . . .' said Mum, sounding tired, as though she'd had to listen to a lot of stress from Dad on the way here. 'We asked in the petrol station, but even the man there hadn't heard of it . . .'

'We've been driving *up* and *down* here, but there's no signs!' he said, partly directing it at the man with the strong eyebrows and the clipboard, as though he was somehow responsible for signage.

'We find a lot of our guests like how hidden away we are!' said Eyebrows, smiling, trying to diffuse the tension, badly.

'We were just worried,' said Mum, 'because we had your suit with us and we knew you'd need it for the show tonight.'

'Look at the view, though!'

'Yes, very nice,' snapped Dad, angrily trundling the wheelie case.

I was furious with them. I had thought this would be the perfect way to show them how great I was as a son – this would be a treat that would cheer them up and make them smile. Dad always seemed to be talking about his friends' sons sending their dads on holiday or how they'd just bought them a new car and how fantastic it all was. This was the thing that Dad could use to show off *back* to them. Finally, after thirteen years of making no money doing gigs on the circuit, I was able to pay for them to stay in a fancy hotel.

I got my things and left for the gig. They were right; there was a chance that I could be late for the show. Despite being occasionally tardy in my regular life, I take great pleasure in being very early for tour shows. I left my parents to it. Frustrated that I wasn't able to make Dad happy.

I got to the gig, and they served me scones with cream and jam, but I didn't know which was the right way to do it in Cornwall, so I just smeared it all together like some sort of pre-prepared scone spread. I put it on social media and people were appalled. I felt like I couldn't do anything right!

The gig was a lot of fun, though, and I returned to the hotel with a spring in my step. Luckily, there is a rule in our family that arguments are immediately forgotten. Walking back to where our rooms were, I knocked on Mum and Dad's door. Mum was getting ready for bed and Dad was already in bed, as was often the case. The windows were closed and the curtains drawn, blocking out the view.

'Everything all right?' I said, pretending the earlier outburst hadn't happened.

'Lovely, thanks,' said Dad. 'We had a lovely dinner.'

'Oh great! Glad you took advantage of being here. They've got a yoga class tomorrow as well, if you like? They say it's open to beginners! You might like it!'

'Hah! We can't do that! We haven't got the right clothes, Tom.'

'You can wear anything you like really – I think they prefer you to do it in bare feet, to be honest!'

'We'll see,' said Mum, laughing. As though I'd suggested, 'Maybe tomorrow we could all go out and try injecting heroin?'

'How come you've got the curtains pulled, anyway? You won't enjoy the view when you wake up!'

'It's a bit warm for your dad, I think.'

'Oh no, Dad! Why don't you open a window?'

'The sea, Tom! It's too loud! It's like a motorway.' Most people would find it relaxing to listen to the waves, but not Dad, not tonight.

The following morning, after breakfast, I asked if they wanted me to try to book out the hot tubs that overlooked the cliffs. There was a wood-fired sauna and a natural lake to swim in. It all looked so lovely. 'No, Tom, I think we're going to have to hit the road.'

Mum had suggested that she would like to go on a bit of a road trip, so I suggested I could organise some hotels to stay in because I'd found some nice ones from the tour. 'Oh, that would be nice,' said Mum as I got my phone out to start booking somewhere for them to stay on this busy Saturday night.

'No, thank you, Tom, I don't want that,' said Dad.

'Why not?' I said, disappointed, wanting to show off that I had enough money to pay for them to stay.

'Because I said so. And we might just head straight back home.'

'Well, Mum just said she wants to go somewhere.'

'No,' he snapped loudly. 'Stop interfering – I can sort out the hotels.'

'Well, I'm just saying I can recommend where to stay . . .'

'I want to book it because I don't know yet where we're going to end up being!'

The tension was rising.

Now I was speak-shouting. 'I know from doing gigs that you might not get in anywhere on a Saturday if you don't book!' I was trying to show him that I had seen the world from my work. I was trying to prove to him that I did know things now; I was trying to protect him.

'You two, stop it!' said Mum, trying to stop us shouting and desperately trying not to cause a scene.

'Why don't you mind your own business?' retorted Dad.

'Because I'm just trying to look out for you, like I've been trying to do for all of my life!'

'What on *earth* are you talking about?!'

'Stop it!' shouted Mum. We were having a row in a public place. We were that sort of family now; the sort of family who had arguments in public. Eyebrows appeared near the table—

'Sorry, guys, can we just keep it down a—?'

'*Yes!*' shouted both Dad and me at the poor man with his clipboard.

Mum and Dad both left soon after. Mum said goodbye, but Dad didn't say anything.

I spoke to them after that night's gig, and they'd ended up going round the Cornish coast and finding the cove where they film *Doc Martin* and even managed to get a night staying in the pub from the series. We didn't mention the argument.

It saddened me that I didn't know how to impress Dad. Or maybe it saddened me that I had tried to do what I thought would impress him, and instead totally missed and it had seemed to make him unhappy. Suddenly, there I was back in the hotel, alone now, the hotel staff looking at me as the man who shouts at his father. What I mourned more than anything was that we couldn't be like the families in films and TV shows who seemed to be able to just live in the moment and enjoy things like this.

Of course, the worst of it all was that I had misunderstood everything so spectacularly. This was the epitome of a poncy pretentious hotel, a hotel that felt it didn't even need a reception desk and offered people fruit smoothies all the time. It was a world my father had never been part of and never been asked to be involved in. Here was me, his pretentious son hellbent on his ideas of what he considered self-improvement, thinking he was making things so much better, when all I was doing was running from myself and pushing the people around me further and further away.

I was trying to force Mum and Dad into coming with me, and then I was surprised that they didn't feel comfortable with any of it. How could I not see that I had become not just a poser, but one who had forgotten who he was? I hated myself for it.

It is foolish to regret, of course. Perhaps that's the hardest thing. If our lives had been perfect and we never had arguments and the risotto was always cooked on time (or cooked at all), then it wouldn't have been us. Perfection is only really for Instagram posts. If my dad had hugged me and looked me in the eye and said, 'I love you, son, and I'm proud of you for bringing me to this hotel,' he wouldn't have been my dad, he would have been a character in a film, probably played by Tom Hanks. That I would have said with moist eyes, 'Thank you, Dad. I love you too,' and not burst out laughing would have meant that I wasn't me either, but some sort of character in a Hallmark film, hopefully being played by Anne Hathaway or Patricia Routledge. Despite my instinct to make everything so posed and performed like the pages of a beautiful cookbook or film, the reality of people being people cannot be overridden.

The Instagram version, where the sun drops below the horizon as we talk about our emotions and then high-five and leap into the air against a glorious sunset, could never be real. The hardest work is accepting that these arguments with my dad are part of the whole, much more real, picture of our lives. All children argue with their parents. Everyone knows this. It is the natural way, the natural clash of parents wanting the best for their offspring and children wanting to find new ways of doing things to prove to their forbears that they are grown-ups just like them. It was our disagreements that showed our love in a way, because they were the moments when we were being our honest selves.

The things I did say, and more painfully the things I was unable to say, play over and over again on the movie projector in my head, tinged at times with terrible regret. These arguments and discords can never be undone now; they were our relationship, our family, our time together despite their faults, but still perfect in their own way. Like a social media page in my mind, these moments will always be there, frozen in time.

Imperfect.

Perfect.

Actually.

'Go into everything with a good heart'

Dad said this to me about maths. He was walking me into secondary school during my first term in Year 7. I was complaining that I didn't really like maths. He told me that I would have to do it whether I liked it or not, so I could do it resentfully, metaphorically kicking and screaming, or I could go into it with a good heart and I might find that I would actually like it. I did really like it after all.

11

Can we go and play now?

Despite feeling like I was about forty-six years old from the age of six, and at times projecting my identity onto legendary screen and stage actress Patricia Routledge, it is only in these last few months that I have found myself standing on my own two feet.

It probably hasn't been as much fun as I thought or hoped it would be. My dad, with his practical, can-do attitude, had protected me from the mundane tasks that make up adult life: he had insisted on taking care of everything.

Recently, the water pressure went in the boiler, and I had to work out how to fix that. I remembered Dad had told me that it was just a case of sidling up to the boiler behind the recycling bins, turning a tap and waiting for the pressure gauge to go up until it reached the red line, but this was terrifying – in my limited world experience, namely some action films, 'pressure' and 'gas' and 'flames' usually combine to make a huge explosion. Since I live in suburbia, where dramatic things tend to be happily shunned, none of these things happened. Instead, it all worked fine. Then I looked at the recycling and felt tired at the thought of breaking down all the cardboard boxes I had used to transport my crockery collection from my mum's house.

The thing about being an adult is there isn't much let up – it's all too much! No sooner have you put one lot of recycling out, you have to bring the bins back in. The clasp on the garage door is broken and there are leaves and cobwebs in the corners where the clasp is and I don't want to put my hand near any spiders, so the clasp is still broken. Every time I see it, I think I must speak to someone about fixing it. Or maybe I should fix it myself – but how? And when? I hardly have time to get scared about the boiler.

There is a problem with the sink in the kitchen and I think I have to get someone round to look at the drains. Something about 'soakaways' and how water runs throughout the house. How could I be so effete that even water – the third most important thing a human needs after air and good lighting – had been something I didn't need to worry about? I guess I always assumed it was something that Dad would inevitably handle.

The light switch in the spare room doesn't work. I've had guests to stay and I've had to give them a candle to light their way like Wee Willy Winky. I feel like I should be able to fix it, but I don't know how. I know I should ask an electrician to come round and fix it, but who? Maybe an electrician would shout at me for wasting their time because I don't know how to fix a dimmer switch and then I'd cry for a week and spend the rest of my days in darkness.

Or worse, what if they were a conman? It would be just my luck to phone someone and for them to be a cowboy, and then I'd have to write in to *Cowboy Builders* (does that programme still exist?). Oh, the shame of being naïve!

In acquiring furniture for the house, I was determined to prove that I could do my own bidding. It was over an antique desk, so it was very much on brand. I found it on an online antique directory. This was the sort of situation my parents would sternly warn me against, and I would feel like a child all over again, because I couldn't seem to make a simple purchase or even take a leap into the darkness without them intervening. Not this time, though. It was my dream desk, and I reached out to the dealer with trepidation – what if he was abrupt with me as well, and thought my questions about inkwells and the smooth running of drawers were a waste of his time? However, in his emails, he was very polite and knowledgeable, and not only that, he was obviously very skilled in restoring antiques. I immediately projected an imaginary future where I would keep in touch and eventually he would invite me to his workshop. It would look just like the one in *The Repair Shop* and I would end up retraining as a French polisher and spend the rest of my days happily wearing an apron, planing planks of wood in some kind of courtyard with lots of nice plants in it. I think I have an overactive imagination.

However, this fantasy future started to crumble after he'd sent his invoice, as the tone of the emails changed and suddenly he was the abrupt person I had always feared.

Any news on the payment?

It seemed so curt! I panicked – I was just so busy with work and that day I had a headache. He had my address – as I'd shared it for the delivery quotation – and I was so scared that he might come round and beat me up! I paid it.

I never heard from him again. I chased on email, politely.

Hellooo, Any news on delivery?

I must have seemed like such a moron. How they must have laughed. There was a mobile number I kept trying, but there was no answer. Of course.

Finally, I got through on the phone and a man answered. 'Oh, hello . . .' I said, timidly, 'It's Tom, I'm phoning about the desk?'

'Ah, yes, have you had any more thoughts about it?' came the man's gentle response.

'Thoughts about it?! I paid you three weeks ago and I've not heard anything about it!'

'Sorry, are we talking about the same desk? The flat one?'

'YES!'

'Well, I've not heard from you since I sent the invoice, so I assumed you must have changed your mind,' he said gently.

Oh God. It dawned on me something had gone awry.

'I think I've been conned.' I read him the details of the invoice, and it was exactly as he had sent it except that the bank details had been changed. Sure, the name didn't match – but I just assumed it was his accounts person. How could I be so naïve?

We worked out that his emails had been hacked, they'd intervened with the invoice to change the account details and I had basically been dealing with a criminal in those abrupt emails, and ultimately in the payment of the funds. It felt like a warning from Dad to remember to use extreme caution when dealing with antique dealers you've found online. 'Don't trust anyone – bastards!' would be the sort of thing he would say. He would also tell me not to be afraid of speaking up to people – 'So what if someone is abrupt? Just be abrupt to them back and they'll soon shut up. You can't go through life being afraid of people, Tom.' Even though he's not here, I can still imagine what he would say. I guess this is the way they arm us to go forward in life, their words echoing through our minds when we need their advice.

Learning these lessons doesn't make someone an adult, though. It just makes you a bit more prepared to deal with things. Over a lifetime, you hope you can grow to have a plan for any given circumstances, and this preparedness is just experience, and I suppose there is no substitute for it: the passing of time combined with the things that we do.

There are certain things I don't expect myself to do, though. Namely, having children of my own. Obviously, lots of same-sex couples have children now, either through adoption or through surrogacy. It was never in my mind, though, growing up, largely because it wasn't an option. Thanks to Section 28, it seemed that same-sex couples didn't exist when I was a child, so the idea of a relationship felt unthinkable, anathema even; the idea of having children an impossibility – how could I have a family when I couldn't even imagine myself with a partner?

What's more, I have always thought children don't like me. Perhaps based on how I felt about myself at primary school and the other kids who didn't want to be my friends. I got it into my head that babies cried whenever they saw me. 'Oh, don't worry! They all cry when they see me,' I would tell the mothers in front of me in the supermarket queue cheerily. 'They can just see the sadness in my soul.'

At other times, friends of mine who had just given birth would think it was a good idea to let me hold the baby. I would reluctantly say, 'Sure,' because it is considered affronting to say, 'Absolutely no, no, thank you.' I would then take the newborn, terrified and suddenly unsure of how to hold anything. I felt like a person holding a prize-winning vegetable for a photograph at a country fair and, mid-photo, realising how ridiculous it is to have a photo with a vegetable. 'Hold the head!' the friend would suddenly bark at me. 'You've got to support the head – their neck isn't strong enough yet!'

I would panic even more and wanted to scream back at them, 'Why have you given it to me if it's not finished yet and the head could fall off?!' but knew if I did say that, the baby would just wake up and start screaming again, confirming my insecurity that babies can see the bleakness in my soul.

A hero of mine has always been Kenneth Williams, as he seemed to have an amazing ability to embrace the sadness he felt about the world. Being markedly different with his pronounced way of speaking and tendency to use long words and intellectual references, he seemed to know that he would be a natural outcast, always bound to be different. Rather than apologise for it or attempt to soften himself to become more acceptable, he seemed to lean into his difference even more. He embraced his feeling of isolation and broadcast the rejection he experienced not just from the people around him, but also the rejection he felt from himself. He talked openly about his feelings of self-loathing, and rather than try to cover up any traditionally 'embarrassing' ailments, he told everyone about them – for example, reeling off beautifully crafted anecdotes about his operation for piles.

It was as though he took ownership of his sadness and his difficulties; they were a way for him to be left alone. He owned who he was and he owned not fitting in. I think I loved him as a child because he was someone I could relate to when I was spending my break-times running away from the other children, taking on the tidying of a school cupboard as a distraction. I loved that there were other people in the world who seemed to feel like they didn't fit within it and spent their time finding ways to reject it or hide away from it. I suppose I wanted to learn from him.

He wrote in his diaries about hating himself despite people loving him. Kenneth Williams, despite his own inner turmoil, was loved by the world around him. People delighted in his stories and his voices and his grandiose musings. He also had a lot of young fans – children loved his voice and he was asked to narrate the animated show *Willo the Wisp* and even presented his own series explaining science to children. Maybe they liked his quirkiness.

So, I've been delighted to accrue some nephews. They sort of crept up on me. It's been wonderful. They're brilliant. Aged eleven, nine and seven. They make a noise when they come into the house and I love it. 'Brace yourself!' they shout back at me through the door when they knock and I gruffly demand, '*Who is it?!*'

They play football and they get upset when they lose or if they get injured. They make pictures and stories and write cards. They are honest too. I once told a story over Sunday lunch and the youngest one said, 'Well, that wasn't very funny.' He is seven years old and was absolutely right. I laughed so much.

One weekend, I thought I'd set them a challenge in the garden to try to introduce them to growing things in the same way my dad had with me. Without me realising, the garden has grown exponentially since I first planted it and the vegetable patch is positively booming. From tiny specks of green poking through the earth to delicate wisps of stalks, they gradually expanded to form leaves attached to tendril-like branches.

I planted a row of chard (Swiss chard and red chard), a row of spring onions and leeks, a row of carrots and then a group of garden peas and two groups of sweet pea. After my battles with the slugs, the leaves seemed to have just about survived so far. The chard now grows tall in broad sweeps of crimson and dark green. The carrots have bold bushels filling the space. In fact, they have all grown much more than I expected. I think I was being typically pessimistic and planted lots of seeds, assuming half of them wouldn't come through. However, they all seem to have come through, and now there is a forest of life.

The garden-pea vines grow in such abundance that they are like something from *Jack and the Beanstalk*. The combination of rain and sun, often in one day as we have seen during the spring, has provided perfect growing conditions. So now I have so much vegetation that they are taking up too much space, and the sweet peas – perhaps too sweet by nature – have to be given extra support to make sure they have enough room. I had put in bean poles and tied them together with old string, but then Linda, my boyfriend's mum, bought me an obelisk to grow the sweet peas up. It looks so elegant in contrast to the other two sets of sticks, which look bedraggled in contrast, but I don't mind, I never wanted the garden to look perfect.

Runner beans are in a converted grow bag sliced across widthways to make two growing pots (thanks, Monty Don via Mum). Thriving are the bay tree, the potted rosemary and the trough of herbs bought for me by Mum and Dad. Thyme and sage and even basil (which I never thought I'd be able to keep alive) are now on hand for using in the kitchen.

Geraniums and a soft-leaved pelargonium are repotted and doing well. The meadow flowers planted at the back of the garden are showing huge promise. They are planted around the sunken trampoline I inherited from the previous owners of the house. I imagine myself one day bouncing amongst the tall poppies, foxgloves and forget-me-nots, with all the gay abandon of Theresa May running through that wheat field.

The bold and brazen hydrangeas at the sides are about to explode now the peonies and camellias have gracefully retreated. A solo rose I was given last year as a gift and that I assumed was dead has come back tall and proud. A pink hydrangea sits in a terracotta pot like a flame among the garden furniture. A wall on one side is covered with moss and ferns, which I like very much, and has now provided a home to a few wild strawberries, which peek out to tickle us.

The slugs still come and I now don't feel so squeamish about dealing with them. It is surprising to me that for a largely vegetarian enterprise like the vegetable garden, a lot of small animals have to be killed to allow the vegetables to prosper.

Two small tomato plants grow tentatively in pots and a lantern gifted to me by Miss Hammond – my friend who once taught me at her Saturday theatre school, the Patricia Hammond School of Dramatic Art, located above a launderette on Belmont Parade, Chislehurst. This good friend of mine has supported me in every beat of my peculiar life, from being an unusual child and an eccentric teenager – at times, dressing up as her butler for her garden parties. Now as an adult, she still seems to understand me better than I do myself.

In the late winter, she texted me to say that she had a gift for me. 'Robert will drop it round!' Robert is not her new butler, but her companion, and as a man who worked for many years in railway timetabling, he runs a very organised retirement. Opening the front door, I discovered six buckets, stacked atop one another, along with fertiliser, packets of seed and six packs of planting potatoes to grow my own.

Miss Hammond remained in their pink car and called out of the window from the kerbside, 'Something for the garden!' with her usual cheeky smile, a silk scarf blowing gently on the wind as she gave a small wave and blew a kiss as Robert drove off with stately order.

My first instinct on closing the front door, holding buckets and potatoes and agricultural equipment, was utter fury. 'Haven't I got enough to do?! Not only am I trying to manage the boiler pressure in this house, but now I've got to work out how to set

up my own potato farm?! Does no one realise how busy I am?!'
It was like I had a chip on my shoulder, but the chips hadn't been
grown yet.

The equipment and the seeds sat by the back door for a few
weeks until the nephews were round. If being an adult isn't just
learning things for yourself but passing on wisdom and knowledge to a younger generation, then maybe these potatoes could
be just the thing.

I'm not much of a teacher to the younger generation. I don't
really carry any authority, seeing as I can barely look after myself,
and what's more, my interests are not the sort of thing that young
people care about – I can hardly introduce a seven-year-old to
Stephen Sondheim's back catalogue.

However, thus far, my attempts to educate them have been based
around the things I like. Yes! At last I can pass on my keenly learnt
skills to a new generation! We started with how to light candles safely.
This was, selfishly, so they could light my scented candles for me.
These football-loving boys seemed to enjoy these new skills, though,
and I was keen to help them get over their fear of the match burning
down too quickly and scorching their hands. 'It's OK! You can blow
it out or you can just shake it and that puts it out?' It might have
looked like I was teaching them to be young arsonists, but I didn't
mind – I needed my sitting room to smell of patchouli!

From this, we naturally progressed to other important skills
like appreciating hand cream. I had been bought a bottle of very
nice hand lotion and there was no way I was going to let anyone
use it without appreciating all the ingredients. I brought it out
into the garden for them to try. 'What can you smell in it?' I
asked like a school ma'am who was taking a class in 'How to act
like a middle-aged gay man'.

'Lime?' they asked.

'Very good! What else?'

'Is there like a herb in there?'

'Maybe . . . What herb do you think?'

'Parsley?'

'No!'

'Can we go and play now?'

'It's basil!'

'Oh.' They sniffed at the hand cream again. 'It's very nice!'

'Of course you can go and play!'

They didn't seem to mind their lesson, though. We have also covered how to present a roast chicken, how to fold napkins and how to lay the table nicely. They never complain that these are boring tasks even though I wonder if they'd probably prefer to be out kicking a football.

We also covered hot beverages, with one of them learning how to make tea, another how to make an espresso and the eldest one learning how to properly froth milk for cappuccinos – and it was oat milk at that, which is much more challenging and he did it perfectly. I was so proud. I'm hoping to one day teach them how to make cocktails and basic sommelier skills, and get them to fix that broken light switch.

I realise that these 'life skills' aren't really useful for any kind of life other than mine. It's not the sort of skills they would learn in the Cubs and Scouts, where rather than lighting a Diptyque candle, they would be learning how to light a fire, and rather than making a cappuccino they would be putting up a tent. These are the skills I would have liked to learn in the Cub Scouts, though – I could have got a badge in 'Fabulous!'

The boys are always very generous to me in that they don't mind these bizarre seminars, and maybe it shows them that it doesn't matter what you are learning about, the world is a better place if you go into it with a good heart. They always do.

Therefore, imagine their delight when I told them we were going to have a potato-growing competition! They looked slightly bemused, but they were still keen.

It was Mothers' Day, and my mum, my boyfriend's mum Linda and my friend Sharon were there with us to help with the planting. Linda used to be Akela in a local Cub Scout group, and this was *exactly* the sort of thing they would do.

'OK, everyone!' said Linda. 'You need to put a bit of earth in the bottom of the buckets.'

'It smells!' said the youngest nephew, honest as ever.

'Yes, that's what nature smells like,' said Linda cheerfully. 'Now we put the potatoes in and some more earth on top.' It was starting to get dark and it was beginning to rain. It was one of those tasks that once you've started, it feels like slightly more work than anyone was in the mood for. Nevertheless, the boys helped each other lift the bags of earth – a bag almost as big as them – to tip some in to cover these potatoes.

'Now what?' they asked.

'Now, we've got to wait for them to grow.'

'Oh,' they said, confused. 'How long do we have to wait?'

'At least ten weeks!' I said excitedly. Ten weeks is a long time when you're in your late thirties, so I can only imagine that it must have felt like an ocean of time to someone under the age of ten.

Dad grew potatoes, but the slugs often munched the leaves. However, some of them did grow and he would proudly bring them in to be boiled up.

The following year he didn't bother but as he was turning the sod, as he'd term the process, he would come in with a fork full of tiny spuds. 'Look at this! Self-sown! They're a gift from God – they just keep coming back'.

It's edifying to remember that the earth sustains us and sometimes gives over and above the effort we put into it. Dad would grow runner beans, which would bloom in tall stalks with orange flowers. The beans were brought in for my brother as they were (and still are) the only vegetable he would eat. Dad tried to grow lettuce, but the slugs, like annoying humans, loved salad too much.

Unfortunately, the boys' labelled buckets of potatoes stayed as dark pots of mud showing no life – not even a whisper of green coming through – for the next month. I knew that they did most of their growing below the ground but this just seemed ridiculous. I worried that I'd have to tell the boys our endeavour had failed and hopefully they'd laugh about it or they'd learn from it that life sometimes goes like that.

However, five weeks after we planted them, I happened to have a look, and young plants had sprung up above the ground. They were small, but there were leaves for sure – they were definitely there!

Ten weeks later, and the plants were huge, like trees growing in these buckets along the side of my shed. 'Not ready yet, Tom,' said Linda. 'Keep watering them – they're still growing below the ground!'

I kept sending photos to the nephews and they seemed excited. A final to the competition was planned.

'The boys want to bring a paddling pool, is that OK?' asked my brother.

'Of course!' I said, though I did feel like maybe they weren't taking the potato party seriously if this was their priority.

When they arrived, I gave everyone a hug and brought them through to see the potatoes, arranged in a line, according to age. Very solemn. Before we could begin, though, I made them pick the pods of peas to have as a healthy snack before lunch.

Despite looking like a huge mass of green leaves and shoots, the garden-pea stalk had not actually yielded that many pods at all. I had been lovingly tending to this plant, and it had given me, in return, twelve things to eat. I dutifully handed them around on a plate for everyone to enjoy. They may have been a bit tough, because I hadn't picked them early enough, but it was an exciting start to the proceedings.

We sat on the new garden furniture I had bought. (The old stuff had worn out. A fox had made a habit of coming to sleep there. It was ruined. Dad was right: I should have put it in the shed when I wasn't using it.) Then we harvested the chard leaves with a view to having them as a side dish over lunch. We picked through the huge red stalks to find any leaves that hadn't been munched on by slugs – most of the leaves resembled some sort of Swiss cheese, full of huge holes. Those slugs really had made their mark. Bastards!

The moment of truth arrived when each of the three boys sat behind their potatoes. A terrible terror swept over me: the plants above ground had grown huge, but there was no guarantee that they would yield many actual potatoes below the earth. It was all very tense. What if I had made all this fuss for nothing?!

'Should we judge the competition on the number of potatoes or on weight?' I asked.

'Weight! Weight! Weight!' said the youngest. We all paused, thinking he had shouted, 'Wait!' before we realised he wanted us to weigh them.

'No, we should do it on numbers or it'll take forever,' said the eldest, calmly and sensibly.

'Yes, OK, let's do that,' I agreed, hastily, also feeling that the eldest (eleven years old) understood his siblings so well he knew that a simple system of counting was essential to prevent any bickering. If there had been an argument, I don't know what I would have done other than to shout, 'Err, behave everyone or there'll be no scented-candle practice!'

Then the digging began. I didn't have a big fork like Dad used, just small handheld forks and shovels for the boys. They wanted to do it one potato bucket at a time. As the eldest began, it was a relief to see loads of potatoes emerging from the earth. Tiny ones and large ones – some so big they would not be out of place in any Spudulike or works canteen.

The middle one went next, but the youngest brother made a start too – he had been waiting ten weeks! Everyone seemed to be very enthralled. Their mum and my brother got involved with the digging too. Eventually, it was decided that they had exhausted the potato supply in the buckets and it was time to see who had won.

They each did their counting. The youngest arranged each potato in a spiral design in order of size. They whispered to me their final tally and I got the prizes. It turned out that the eldest and the middle one had exactly the same tally of thirty-three. I immediately felt bad for the youngest one who only had twenty-six. However, he didn't seem to mind at all. Noticing that his brother had fallen behind, the eldest gave him some of his. This messed up the system, but who cares! They all got the same prize anyway – a bag of sweets and a round of applause and a pen my mum had bought them on holiday in Greece. (The middle one doesn't like sweets, though, and prefers vegetables, so he got a head of broccoli, which he immediately ate raw. Perhaps I wasn't all that unusual as a child after all.)

The paddling pool was taken from its box. Alfie had to use a knife to open it, and I was annoyed that he'd used my best knife but then reminded myself that it didn't matter. It had to be inflated with a motor and since the plug sockets were in the kitchen, the paddling pool was inflated there and nearly knocked my salad display and my favourite serving platters off the work surface. But I didn't care; we were all together and the sun was shining.

Placed in the middle of the garden and filled with water, the boys amused themselves by running and jumping into it – which must have hurt since it was only about a foot deep. They also wore swimming goggles, which felt even more extravagant. I approved. They played happily while I boiled potatoes and barbecued a salmon.

I take ages to make food and the middle boy came to talk to me while I was fussing around with the chard, trying to make it perfect like something Nigel Slater might write about in the *Observer*. 'What are you doing?' he politely asked.

'Oh, just chopping the chard for us! Can you believe so much of lunch was grown in the garden?!'

'I know, it's great!' he said, walking over to the stove to look at what was happening there – namely the boiling of potatoes. I was instantly concerned that he might burn himself and wanted to tell him to get away. I didn't know I could be so parental! Then I realised that he was nine and not a toddler, so was able to make judgements for himself.

Eventually, it was all ready to be served, especially the salmon, which I had put on the barbecue and forgotten about. Mum called out to say, 'The salmon! It's on fire!' which was true, but I tried to pass it off as 'rustic cooking'. We ate together and everyone remarked that the potatoes had been a huge success.

I was learning to relax and be in the moment with everyone – we were here, all of us, together, and that was all that mattered. None of us had to pretend to be anything other than ourselves. Over six months since Dad left us, we were emerging from our grief as a new unit: this was my life now, my home, my family.

In this moment, a pang of guilt hit. In being happy, it panicked me that we were somehow moving forward and leaving Dad behind in that sad winter day when he left us. I wondered if he would recognise us all sat there, the garden changed so much since he saw it, complete now with meadow flowers and a burgeoning vegetable patch – the house now in summer and no longer in the winter when he died. How he would have been confused to see the people he knew so well, sitting together, carrying their grief like a secret stone – growing potatoes to try to desperately hold on to him.

The eldest boy lay on the grass after lunch and looked up at the clouds. 'There's so many shapes up there! You can imagine all kinds of things. I can see a pirate!'

For me, after the warm spring and summer of 2020, when we were all forced to stay home as part of the first lockdown, the world will never quite return to normal again. I came to appreciate how quiet the world could be. Amongst all the fear and sadness of the pandemic, there was space to be still, to see who we were and to appreciate the world we were living in. Dad would show me his vegetable patch and how it was coming along or he would sit in the chair on the patio, reading the paper, topless in the baking sun. Sometimes, he would tell me excitedly about the family of tiny birds who had come to live in the small bird-house he had nailed to the back fence. I'd come and sit with him and we'd talk. We learnt to enjoy these small pleasures and quiet moments during that time. I was still yearning to be back in the world before everything had been paused, and longed to do my work and to see friends, but slowly I came to realise that none of that mattered because everything I needed was right there.

Since no one was allowed to travel during the first lockdown, the sound of the traffic and the occasional airplane overhead were silenced. The world was beautifully quiet. I think I had always assumed that we, as humans, lived in built environments with trees, plants and animals fitting in around the edges, but as I think we all came to realise, the natural world *is* the world, and the places we call home are really just tiny corners of a forest we have merely borrowed. We cannot deny the natural order of things – the life that comes to be, the changing of the seasons, the tall trees that were here before us and will probably be here long after we are gone.

It was a Tuesday morning when Dad walked down the front path and stood in the road. 'Listen to that,' he said, still my teacher. 'You can hear the birdsong so clearly. It goes on forever.' I stood with him and heard the birds echoing around all the trees of suburbia, the world I had grown up in, the world I thought I knew so well, transformed into an eternal aviary.

I had spent so much time trying to find Dad, and at times trying to run away from him, but at the last moment, I came home to Bromley. Not just to his home that I lived in for so many years, but also to the home I'd started to create, complete with my own garden and my own life, right where I started, in a suburbia where we both felt like we belonged.

I feel like I spent all that time running, thinking I needed to be far away before I could be myself – finally free of his love and able to make mistakes and fail all on my own in America or in Japan or trying to forge a career that couldn't have been more different to his. In truth, it was only when I came home that I understood myself. And in understanding myself, I realise I understood him too. He is right here in the vegetable patch, in the time I make to spend with my new families, in the things he said to me, repeating in my head, 'You can never have too much love.' I had run away, but here in the garden he'd found me, and found me no longer a boy but now a grown-up man myself.

Epilogue Epistle

Hi Dad,

You all right? Just finished the book. I wrote about how strange you would find it to see us all sat in the garden here at my house, having a barbecue, but still struggling with our loss. It made it sound so poetic, as though you would be some gentle ghost hiding behind the plants. I know full well you would say, 'What a load of bullshit! Stop worrying about me and get on with having a great time.'

You won't be surprised to know that I left the finishing touches of the book to the last minute and had to ask for an extension on the deadline. I know! Typical of me to always be late, always rushing around. I can see you rolling your eyes at me, slumped on the sofa in the TV room, wearing your joggers, your baggy jumper and your slippers with the paint marks on them. You were resigned to the fact that I would be late for everything, and I'm sorry for that. I remember you trying to tell me that I should give myself plenty of time so I don't end up rushing around, but I don't seem to be able to absorb it. 'Give yourself a chance and break a big task down into manageable chunks so you can get it done and then you can relax – that's what I do.' I know, I know.

But it is hard writing a book about you when you've only just gone and bleedin' died!

As I finish writing it, I can hear you say, 'Shall I go down the road and get us some fish and chips, or what?' I'd come with you to get them but you'd insist on paying and that nice lady at Salisbury's chip shop would smile as she hands them over the counter. You never ordered enough chips, though – I always said that. Mum would stay at home and heat up the plates and butter the bread. We'd blast the heat in the footwell of the car to keep them warm on the way home. I loved being us, all together. I loved it during the pandemic, when people weren't allowed in the house, and James and his girlfriend came round and we set up a table in the front garden. We would end up eating fish and chips by the bins. Looking back, it couldn't have been further from the fussy, over-the-top meals I'd always attempt, hellbent on presentation over everything else. Fish and chips like that was so much better than any meal I could have done.

The real reason I was late with the book was that I kept putting off writing this letter. I've spent the last six months pleading with God. 'Oh, surely I can have just one phone call? Even murderers get that in prison!' But the rules don't work like that, and I am left behind here, trying to make sense of what I would have liked to say. You gave me so much advice that I am still remembering it.

'Hurry up for gawd's sake!' I can hear you saying to me now, never one for sentimentality, telling me to get on with it and write this last bit of the book so I don't hold the readers up.

OK, I'll hurry up, everyone – sorry. I think I always overcomplicated things, didn't I? Overthought things at times. You'd tell me to stop worrying. 'You're not happy unless you've got something to worry about!' I worried that I didn't make sense to you when I was off cavorting around, trying to live this queer performer's life – whatever that even means.

We were different, weren't we? In lots of ways. You always accepted me, though. Our differences taught me what love is: it doesn't matter how we expect it to be, it just is. I lived with you for so long because I wanted to be around you and Mum, and that was it. I just wanted us to be together. In life, that's all any of us have, isn't it? Each other.

You taught me to drive, but you knew I was too nervous really, so you always gave me lifts – it didn't matter where I was going or at what time. I would have been late for my whole life if you hadn't offered to give me a lift. A lift in so many ways!

Anyway, I won't keep you (that's what you'd say on the phone, by the way). What's the traffic like up there? Are you complaining about the roadworks? Are there traffic wardens? I hope not. Oh, and you should see the garden here! I've got peas and carrots but the bastard slugs keep coming for the leafy vegetables. Not as many runner beans as you, though. The potatoes – 'tayters' as you would call them – have been abundant, and I think the boys enjoyed their competition. You would have loved that day. So many potatoes it almost makes up for the lack of chips.

That's all, the end, OK? Sorry, it's a bit of a ramble this letter, isn't it? Probably a bit of a mess of thoughts and things, but that's life, isn't it? We are all a bit of a mess sometimes – still loveable, though, right?

Oh yeah, and who is going to give me a lift to the station now, eh? Charming!

Love you always,

Tom x

Acknowledgements

This book would not have been possible without my long-suffering editor, Myfanwy Moore, who has put up with my strange schedule throughout this process. To the team at Hodder Studio, including Tom Atkins, Vickie Boff and Veronique Norton, thank you for putting this book out there.

Thanks as always to my manager, Flo Howard, for making everything possible, along with Lily Morris, Katy Helps and the always dedicated team at the mighty Off The Kerb.

Thanks to my friend Eleanor Thom for the late-night chats and advice and thoughtful insight. Thanks to Amy Annette for solving the last pieces of the puzzle. Thanks to Phil Jerrod, whose encouragement still rings in my ears. I would not have been able to write this without the inspiration of my family – my brother James, Tash and the boys, and my mum Irene – for their ongoing strength. Thanks also to Alfie for getting me on the plane that day, for always listening and always having my back.